UNLAYERED

LIFE: THROUGH THOUGHTS & QUOTES

PRIYANKA DEWAN

INDIA • SINGAPORE • MALAYSIA

ISBN
Paperback: 979-8-88749-918-5
Hardcase: 979-8-88749-931-4

Dedication

To Anuj, my husband, the wind beneath my wings.

To Ayansh and Amayra, my two beautiful children, for rendering me strength to become a better version of myself.

My parents and sister for making me what I am.

Acknowledgments

Every life that touches yours has a reason. Every circumstance that you encounter has a meaning. Every adversity helps you grow better. Every triumph gives your life a resolve. Through these heartfelt and soul-touching renditions, I thank everyone who has made me live through any of these emotions, for it was in these moments that I became what I am… I emerged and am still emerging.

I sincerely thank my readers for choosing this book. I believe everything in life has a purpose and things come to you at the opportune time if you have unwavering faith. I sincerely wish that you have picked this book when your soul desired it the most, for nothing gives an author more satisfaction than making a difference to any life that got connected through the medium of this book.

A very special thanks to Mr. Aman Lekhi, Senior Advocate, Supreme Court of India, and former Additional Solicitor General of India in the Apex Court, who is my powerhouse of motivation and inspiration. Appreciation from him brings out the best in me!

I would also like to acknowledge with much appreciation the team of Notion Press for helping me realize my dream in such a seamless manner.

Acknowledgments

Author's Note

We are all made up of a melange of emotions, each a distinct one. I wouldn't say positive or negative, for it derives that character because of what we attribute to it. Putting together those broken pieces of your soul will never be easy, but trust me, it gets easier when you realize that it's not insurmountable. For long, my happiness meant to keep everyone around me happy! Whether personally or professionally, I thought that was the way of life and it became my natural choice. It took me long to have that realization that, that elasticity in me was beginning to hurt as I was stretching without being happy myself. Neither did my stretching less seem a plausible option to them, as obviously they were used to a certain "me," and with that limitless guilt, nor did it work with me. So I began stretching even more, until I couldn't bear the burden of it anymore.

I confess it was very late in life that I realized that I am the most important person of my life; that I have a right to choose my happiness over those of others without feeling guilty. And it's really not that they are at fault or for that matter you are. It's just that by being entangled in that web of expectations, both are in an endless chase of the unknown. Every relationship takes a different shape through different phases of your life. The expectations, the want from them is a fluctuating phenomenon. And maybe it is too much to expect the other to understand you through your tribulations, maybe it is unfair on you to feel wanted;

likewise, maybe it is unfair on the other to bear the burden of your expectations!

It's never too early or too late for anything in life. Your self-realizations happen when they are meant to be. It's just that sometimes in this fast pacing life, in order to cope up with those mundane activities, we forget to cogitate to find out the purpose of our lives. We become oblivious to our blessings in those ups and downs of life. There's nothing to feel guilty about any of it though because that's why we are humans. We only need to reminisce that we have traveled lifetimes to be here… in this journey… in this moment. After a fall, rise is the only consequence. The life we are living is our will, the destiny that's destined is our choice.

It was in this transition that I happened to write these soulful quotations. I call them soulful because these renditions helped my restless soul settle in the body for which it was made. My creator unveiled me to me and helped me realize the power of "me" that I hold within me and I just kept pouring all of these straight from the heart. Not that I would say that I have changed, because I earnestly feel no one changes from what their basic constitution is, it is just that one learns to conquer those inner conflicts and make a better choice of living their lives! Since I wrote them I have myself visited them often for they make me feel more empowered, more strengthened, more healed, and more evolved. In my moments of those gigantic gushes of inner conflicts, I draw upon these to settle me, to calm me, to help me resurrect and make me a better version of myself, which I am so capable of.

This book is an endeavor to reflect the reflections of various facets of life in a relatable manner… close to heart and closer to soul; the intent is to give a literary treat to the readers on everyday aspects that intrigues the spark of thoughtfulness: find your own strengths and celebrate yourself! I earnestly hope that this book has come to you in your moments of transition… for it will mark its mark at its best then!

Let your journey embark…

Liberate yourself from chartering the rigmarole of your life in this moment. We are oblivious to the fact that the quest to capture the certainties in the uncertainties only makes life more uncertain. After all the rising sun is a reminder that new beginnings are but natural.

Conquer those inner conflicts and rise above your fears. A fall is an occasion to resurrect.

Remember, the breath you are breathing is just yours… know your power.

The vastness would lose meaning if the sky and sea were to meet.

Who says a tree without leaves isn't nature's glory.

You are beautiful… beautiful with all your unique imperfections!

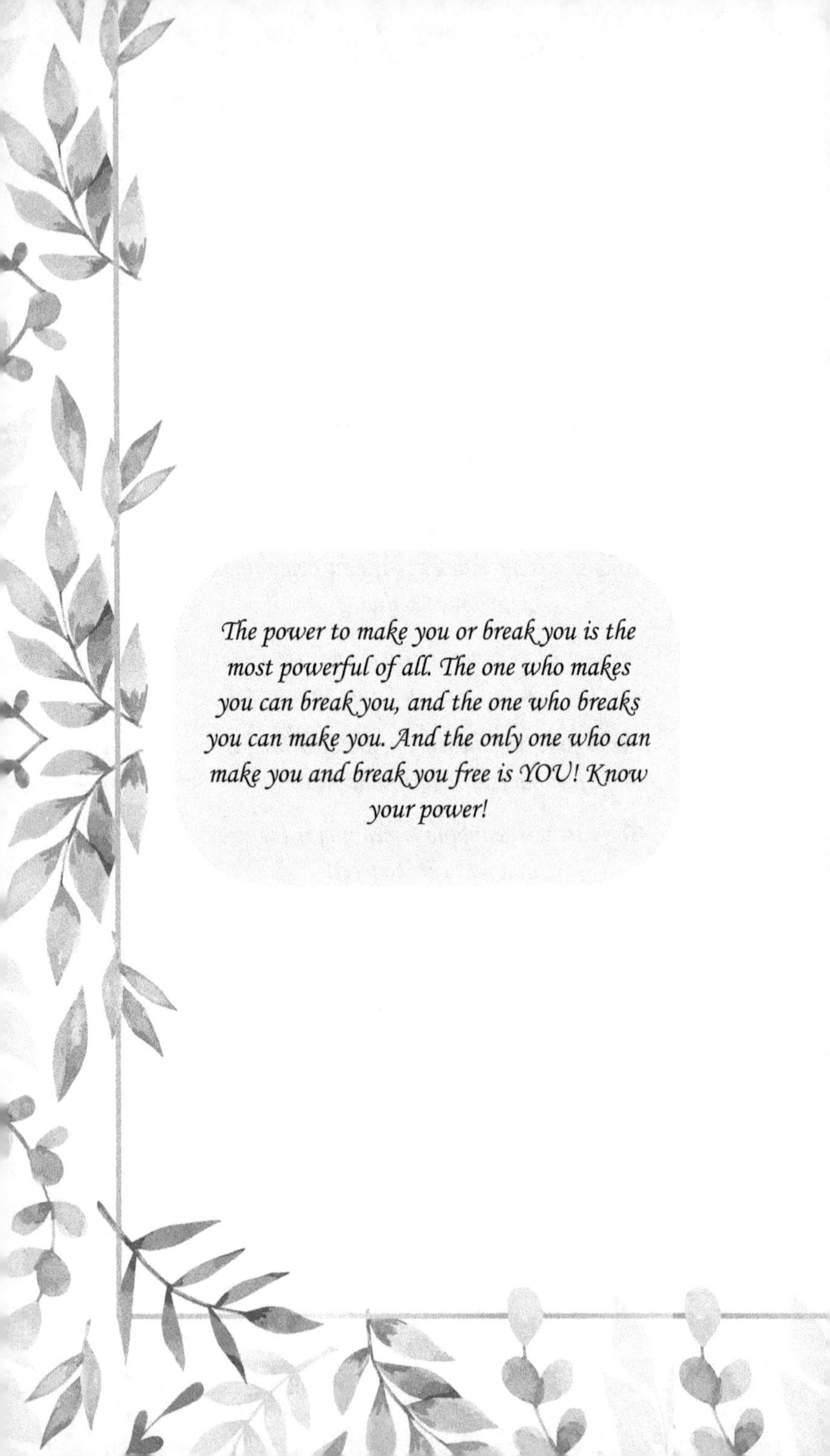

The power to make you or break you is the most powerful of all. The one who makes you can break you, and the one who breaks you can make you. And the only one who can make you and break you free is YOU! Know your power!

If it's about explanation, it's not love

If it's not about healing, it's not love

If it's about judgment, it's not love

If it's not about strength, it's not love

If it's about justification, it's not love

If it's not about caring, it's not love

If it's not about understanding, it's not love

If it's not about support, it's not love

If it's about ruining, it's not love

If it's not about growing, it's not love

If it's about accusing, it's not love

If it's not about progressing, it's not love

If it's about winning, it's not love

If it's not about warmth, it's not love

If it's about scars, it's not love

Choose well!

Why ruminate perspectives to the sun rising or setting in, when both are transcendent in their own ways.

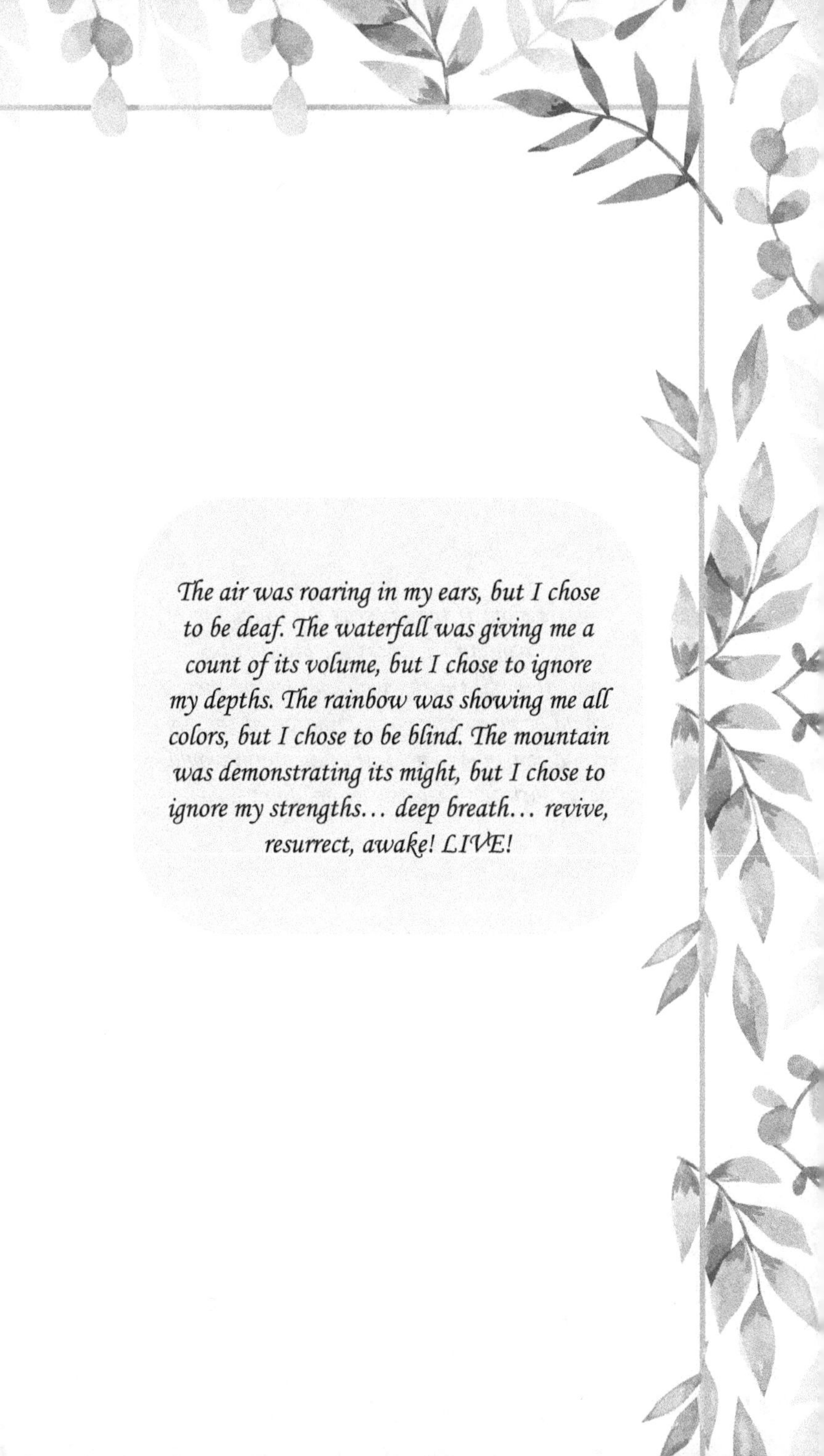

The air was roaring in my ears, but I chose to be deaf. The waterfall was giving me a count of its volume, but I chose to ignore my depths. The rainbow was showing me all colors, but I chose to be blind. The mountain was demonstrating its might, but I chose to ignore my strengths… deep breath… revive, resurrect, awake! LIVE!

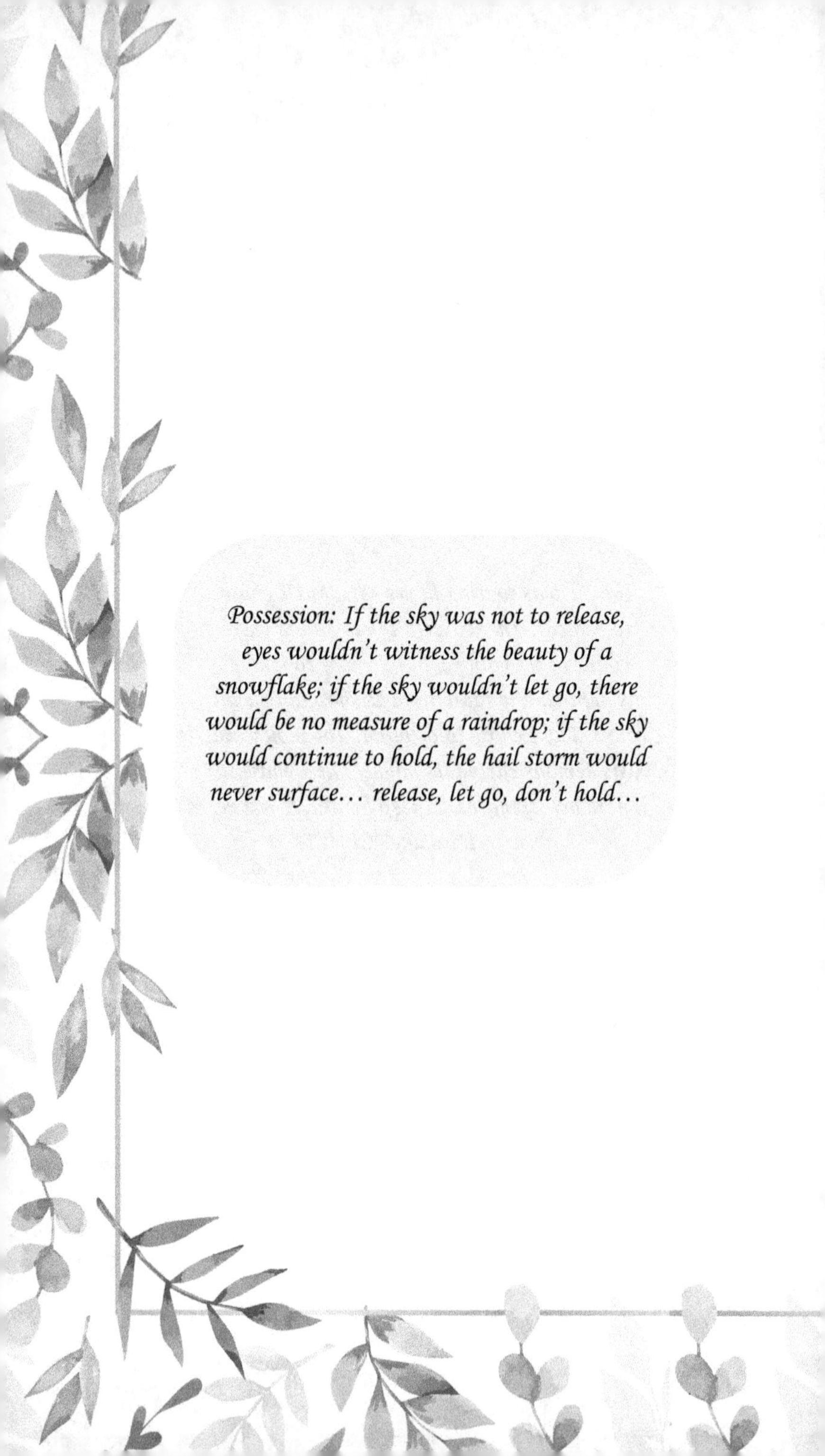

Possession: If the sky was not to release, eyes wouldn't witness the beauty of a snowflake; if the sky wouldn't let go, there would be no measure of a raindrop; if the sky would continue to hold, the hail storm would never surface… release, let go, don't hold…

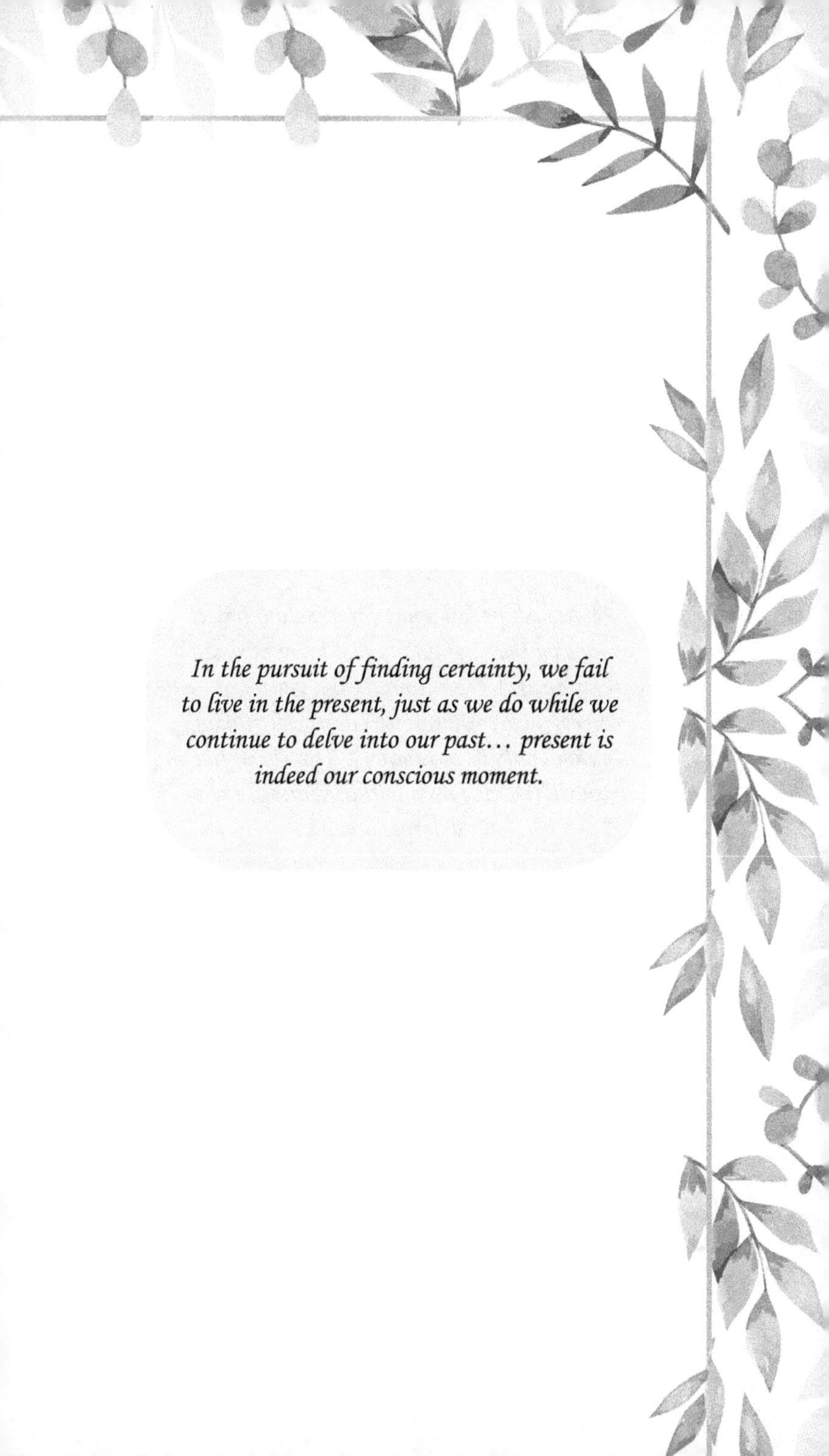

In the pursuit of finding certainty, we fail to live in the present, just as we do while we continue to delve into our past… present is indeed our conscious moment.

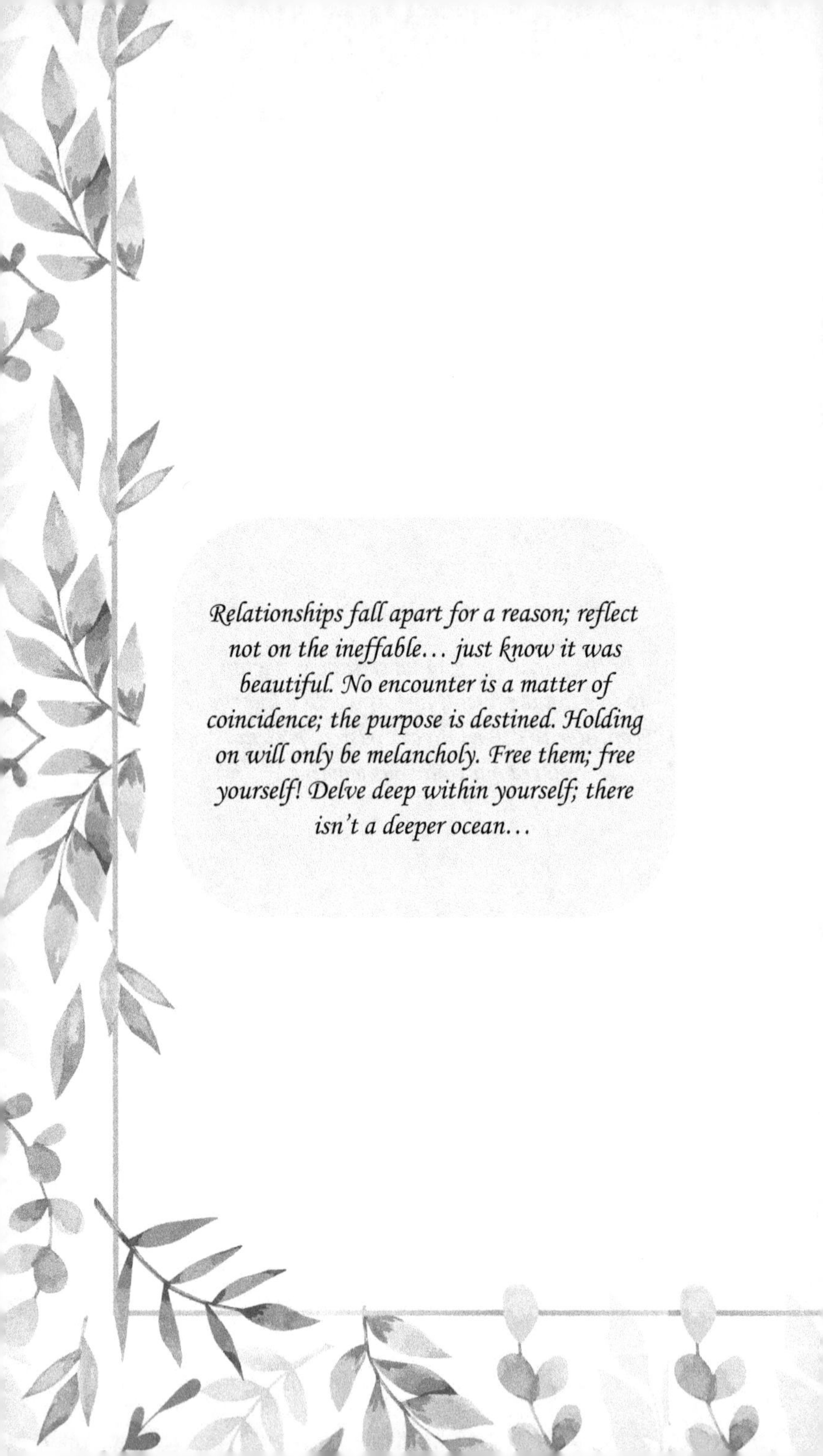

Relationships fall apart for a reason; reflect not on the ineffable… just know it was beautiful. No encounter is a matter of coincidence; the purpose is destined. Holding on will only be melancholy. Free them; free yourself! Delve deep within yourself; there isn't a deeper ocean…

The decision to be "ordinary" or prefix it with "extra" is just YOURS!

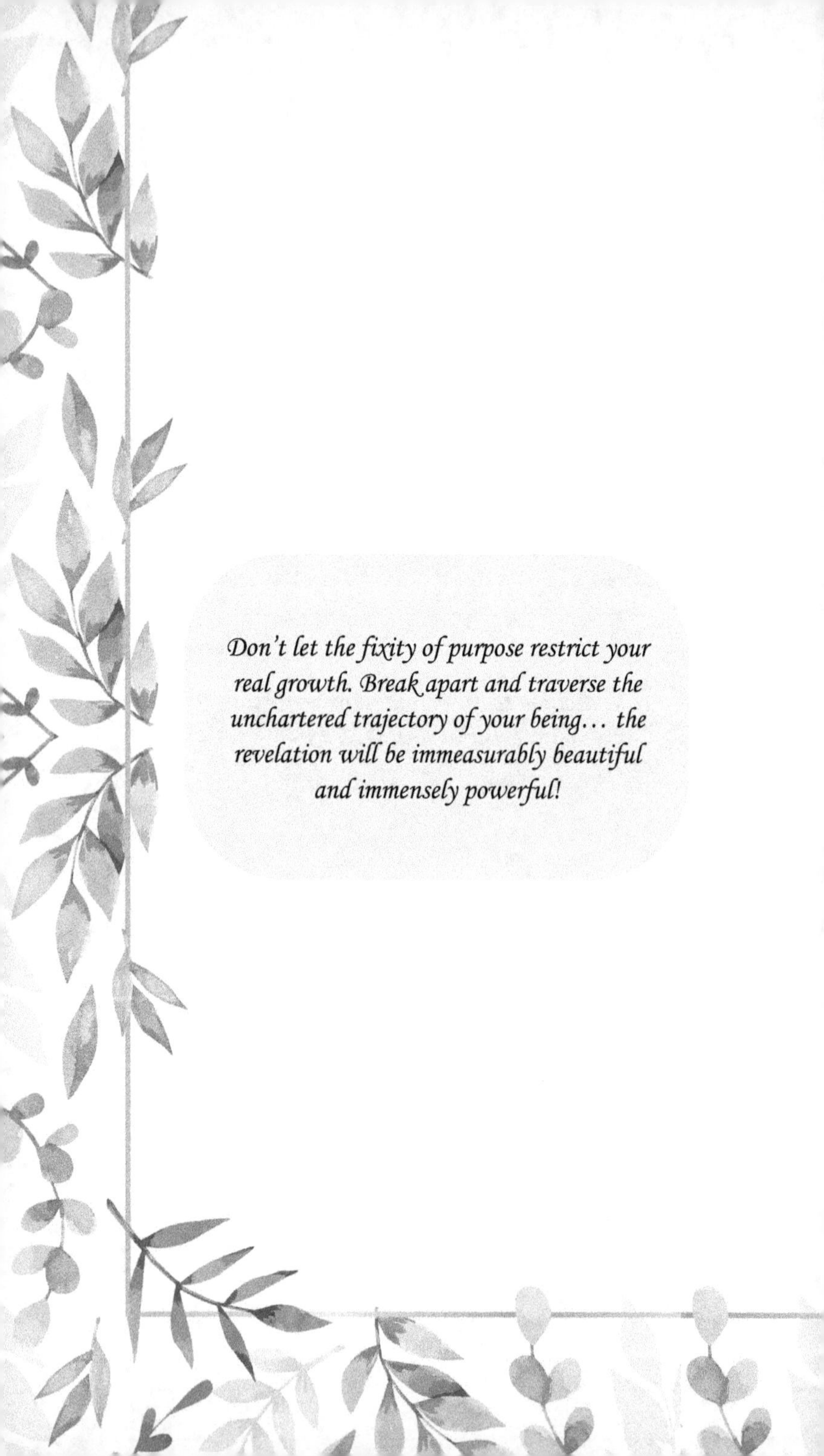

Don't let the fixity of purpose restrict your real growth. Break apart and traverse the unchartered trajectory of your being… the revelation will be immeasurably beautiful and immensely powerful!

Dream a dream as though it was a reality
and live reality as though it were a dream!

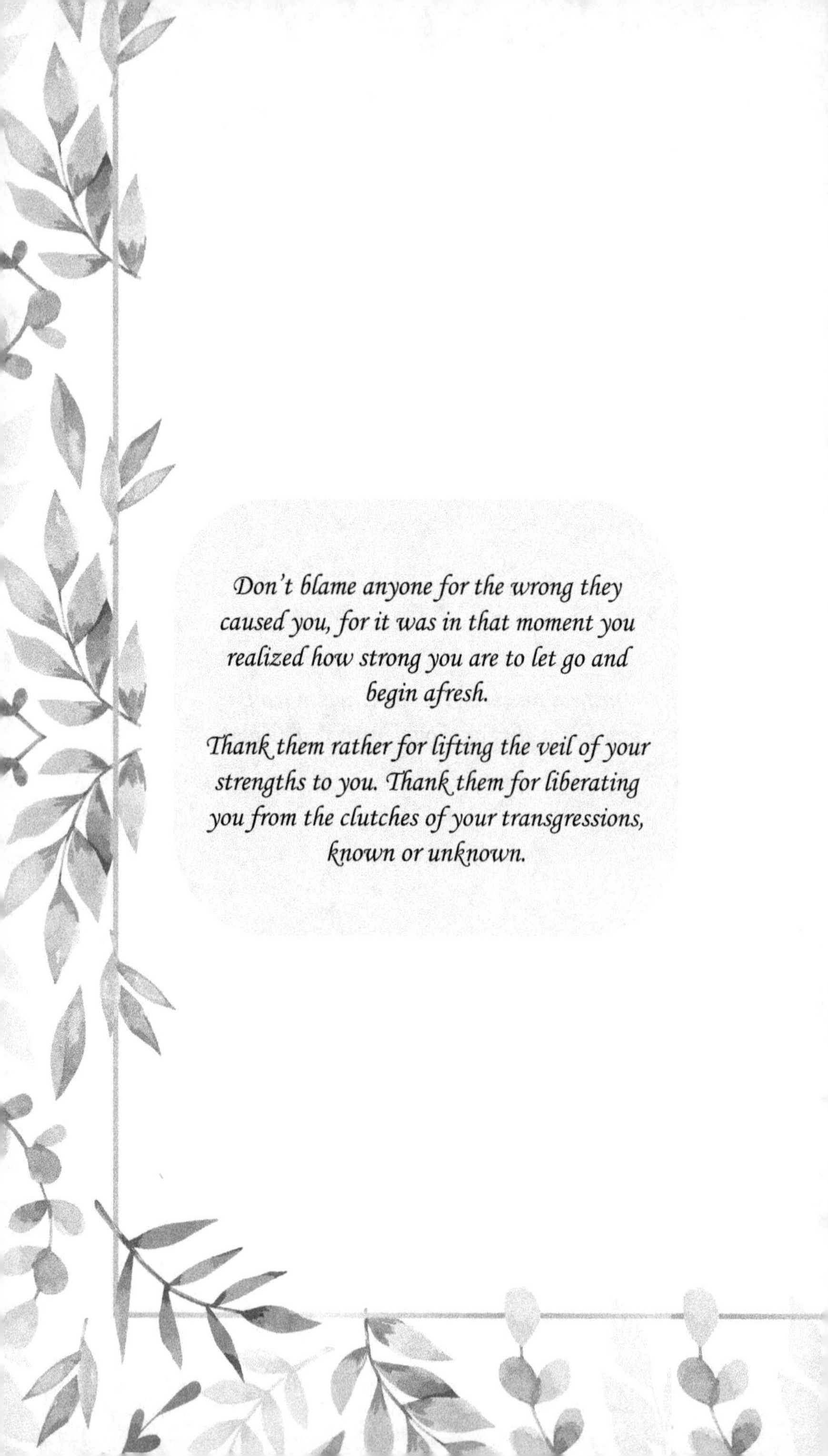

Don't blame anyone for the wrong they caused you, for it was in that moment you realized how strong you are to let go and begin afresh.

Thank them rather for lifting the veil of your strengths to you. Thank them for liberating you from the clutches of your transgressions, known or unknown.

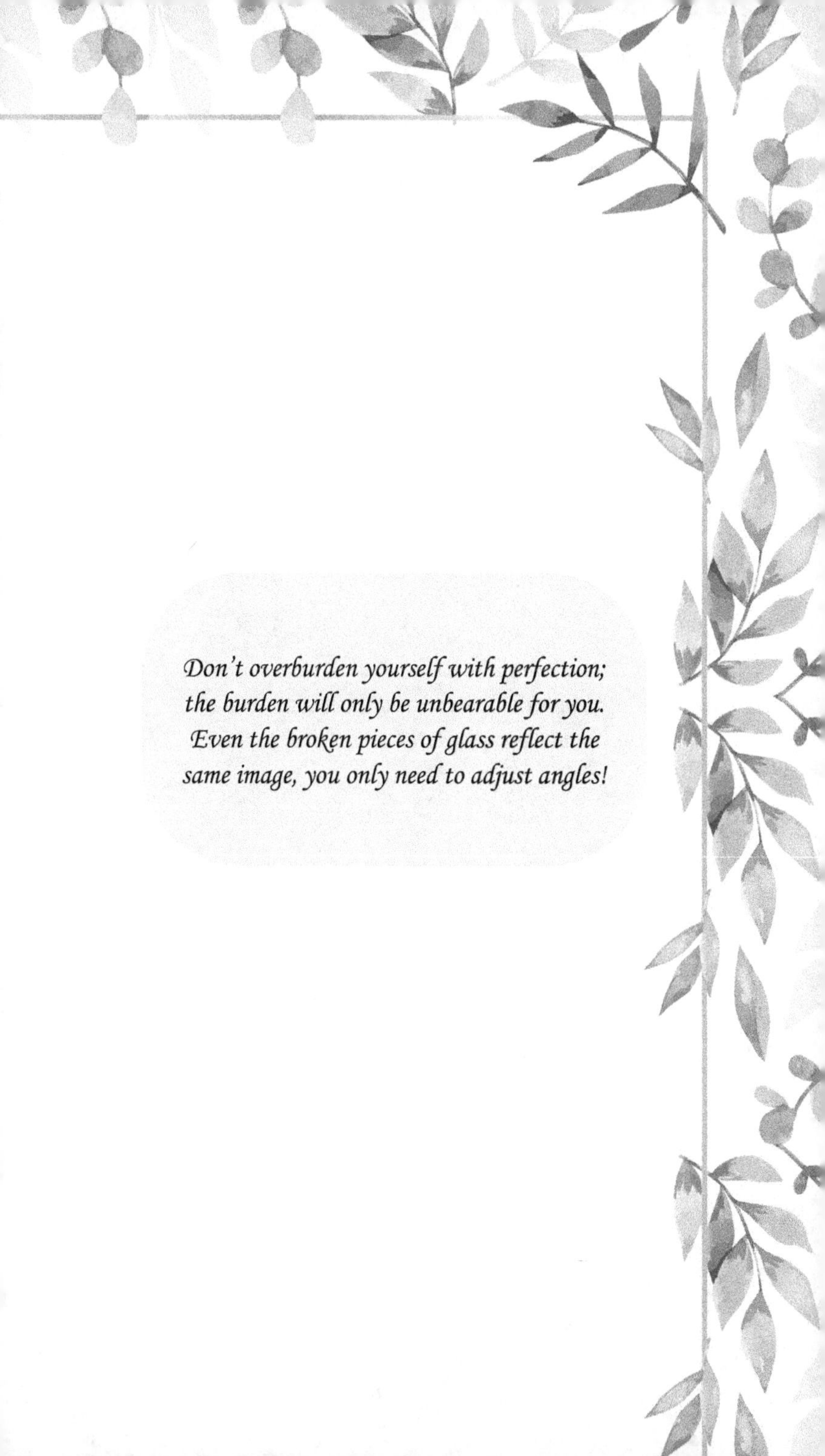

Don't overburden yourself with perfection; the burden will only be unbearable for you. Even the broken pieces of glass reflect the same image, you only need to adjust angles!

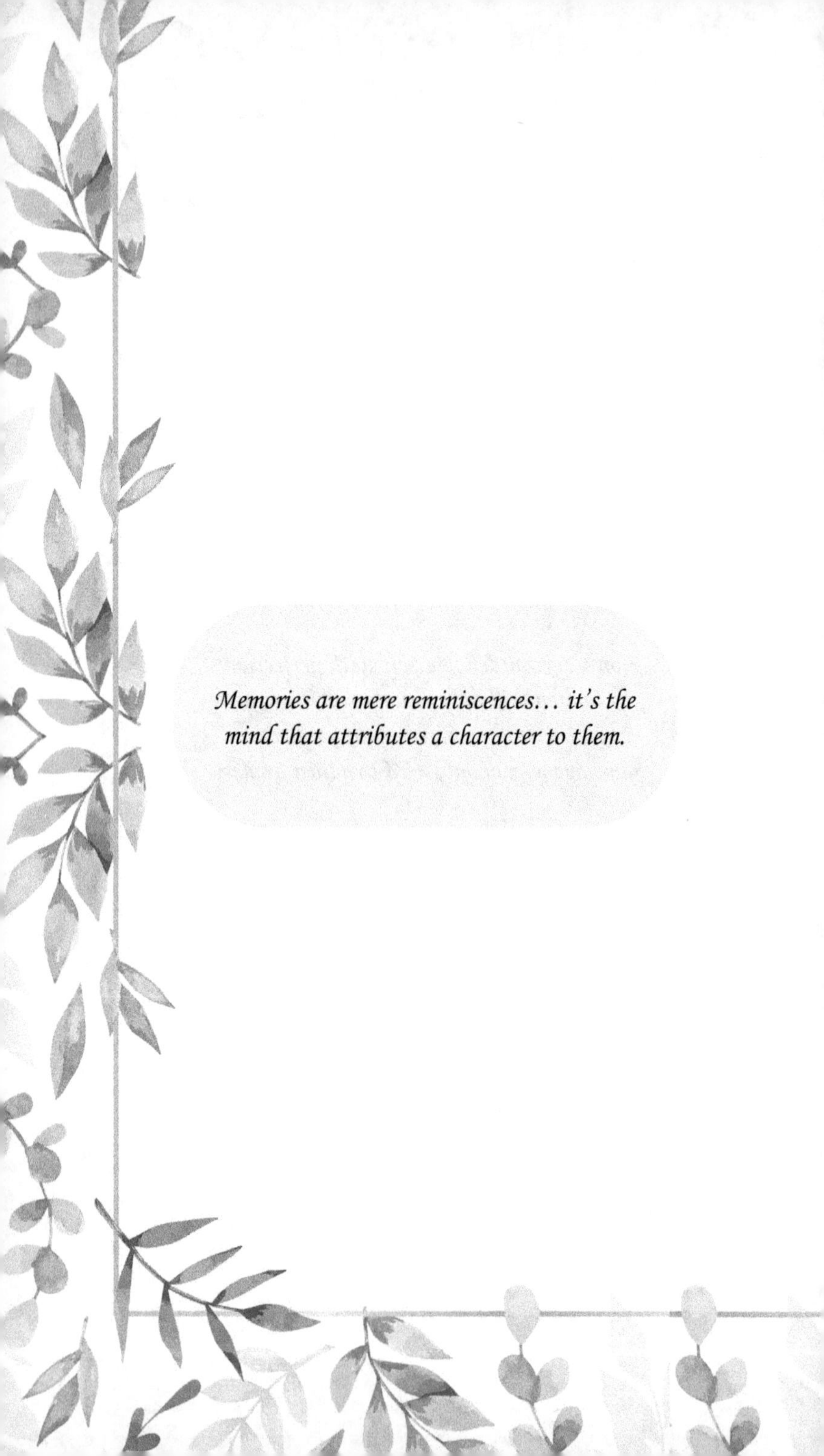

Memories are mere reminiscences… it's the mind that attributes a character to them.

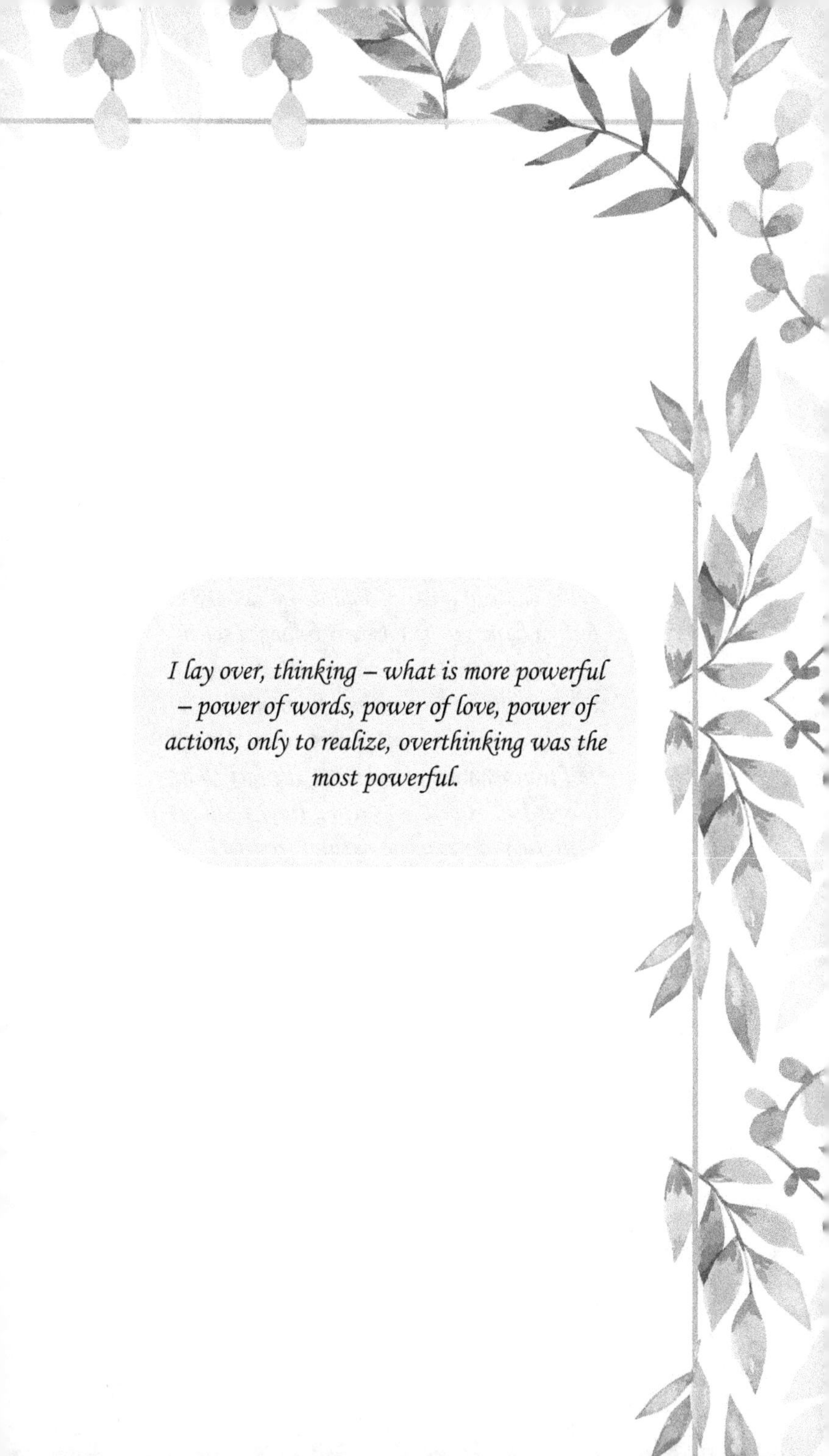

I lay over, thinking – what is more powerful – power of words, power of love, power of actions, only to realize, overthinking was the most powerful.

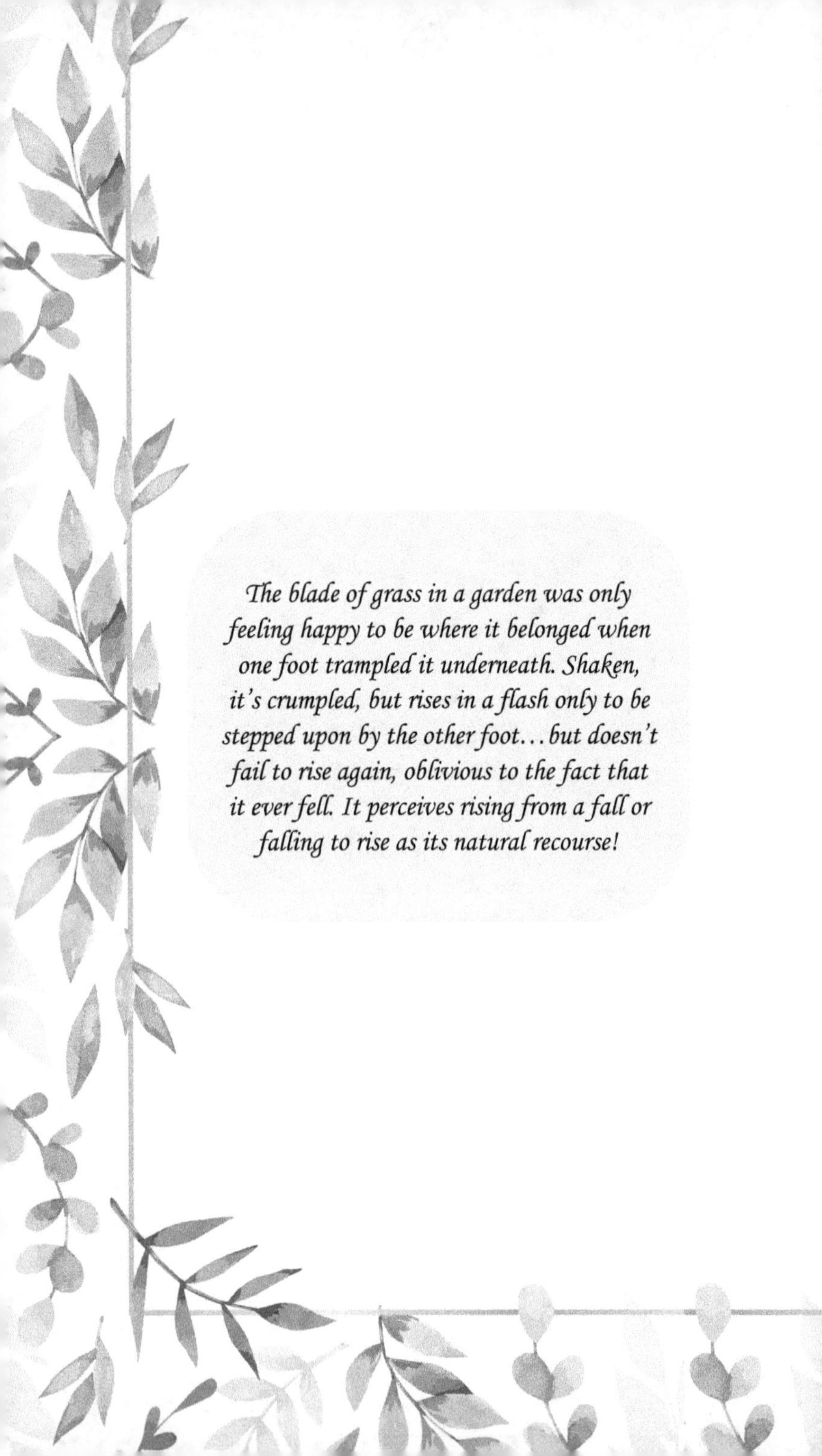

The blade of grass in a garden was only feeling happy to be where it belonged when one foot trampled it underneath. Shaken, it's crumpled, but rises in a flash only to be stepped upon by the other foot... but doesn't fail to rise again, oblivious to the fact that it ever fell. It perceives rising from a fall or falling to rise as its natural recourse!

Break free to be you… and that makes the most beautiful YOU!

Illuminate from within that your light shines its brightest shine. Remember, a star shines even on the darkest of nights only because it chooses to shine!

Contour the vacillating mind to an oscillating rhythm, and that determines your strength.

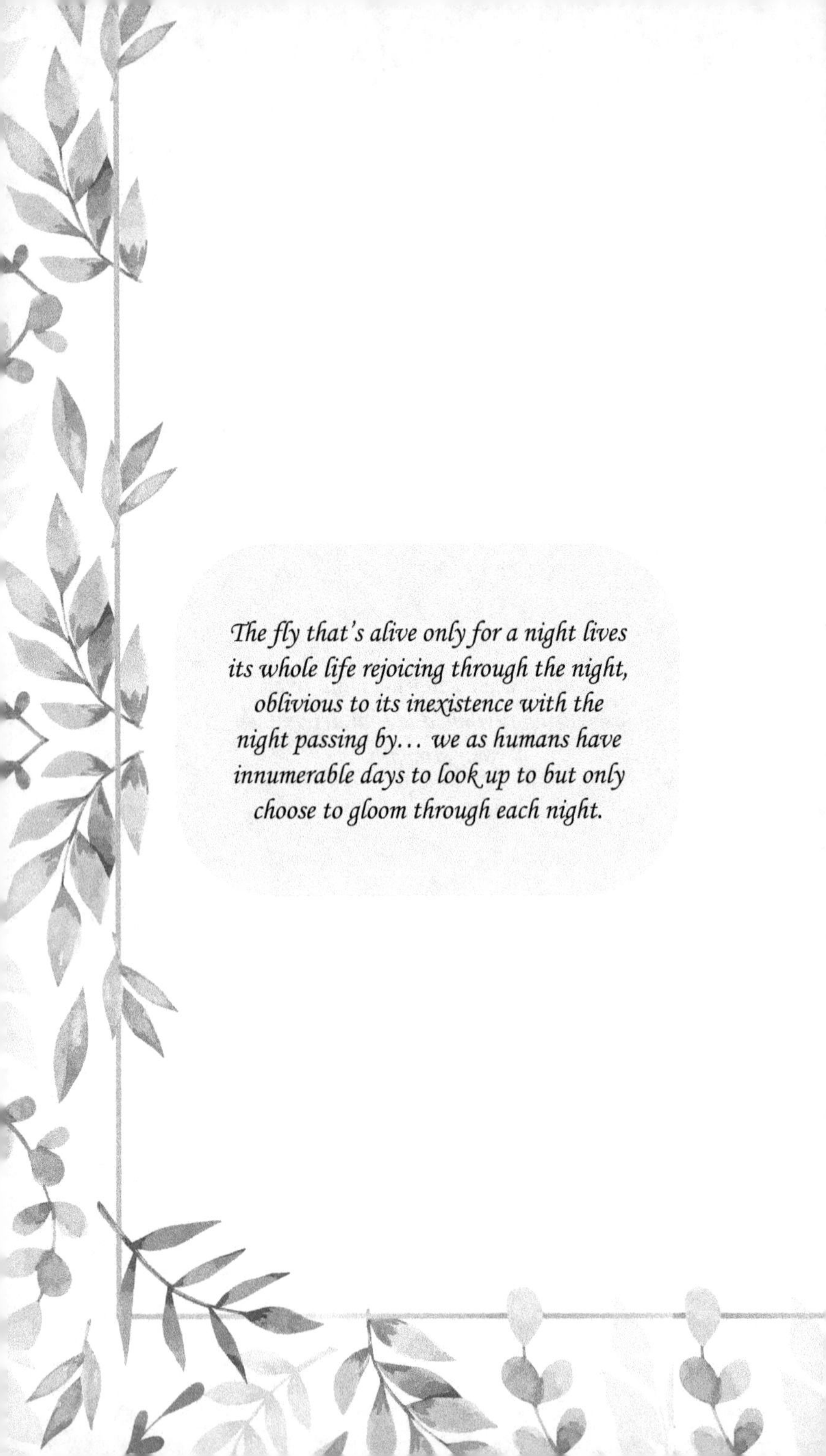

The fly that's alive only for a night lives its whole life rejoicing through the night, oblivious to its inexistence with the night passing by… we as humans have innumerable days to look up to but only choose to gloom through each night.

The burden of expectations, weighs only you down.

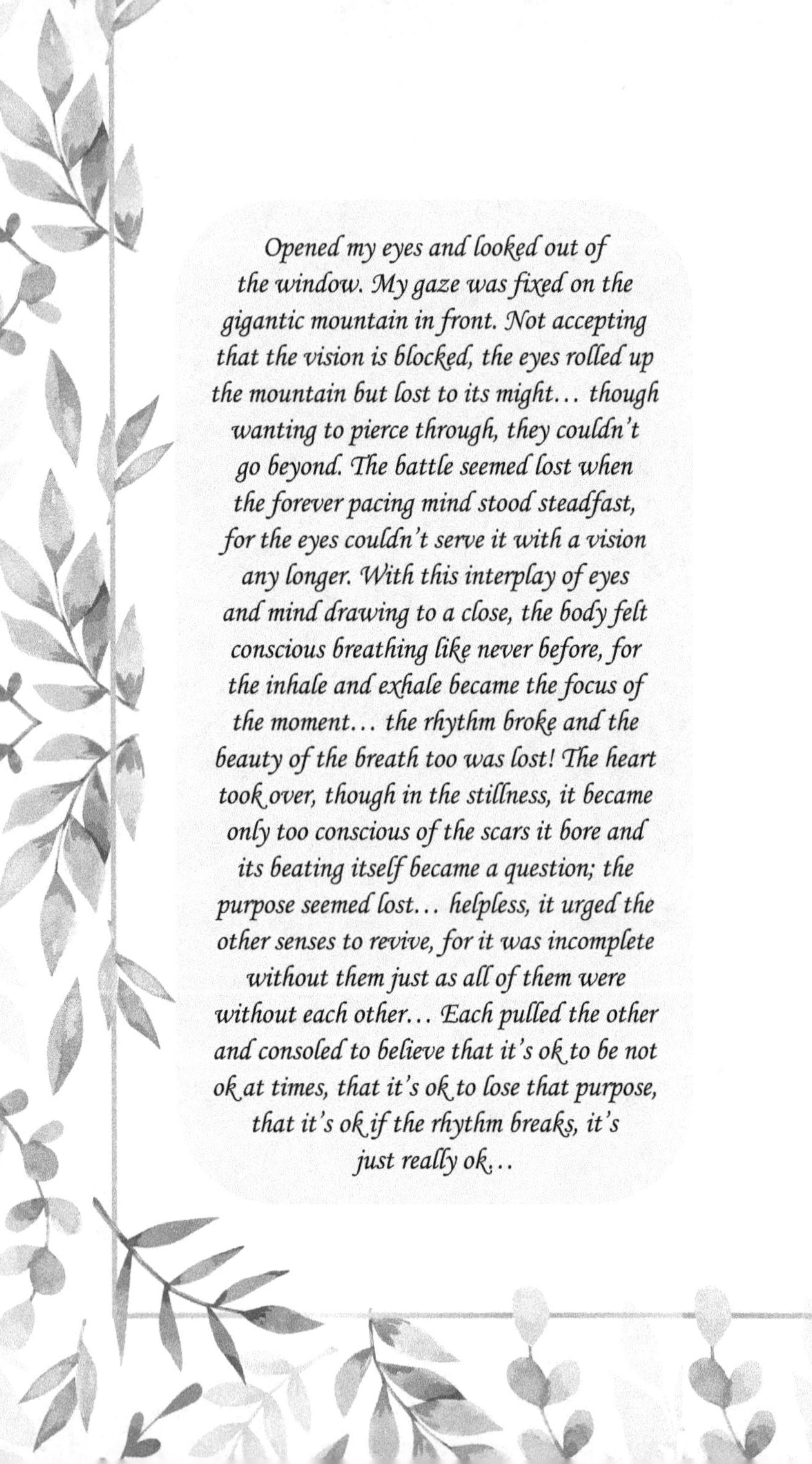

Opened my eyes and looked out of the window. My gaze was fixed on the gigantic mountain in front. Not accepting that the vision is blocked, the eyes rolled up the mountain but lost to its might… though wanting to pierce through, they couldn't go beyond. The battle seemed lost when the forever pacing mind stood steadfast, for the eyes couldn't serve it with a vision any longer. With this interplay of eyes and mind drawing to a close, the body felt conscious breathing like never before, for the inhale and exhale became the focus of the moment… the rhythm broke and the beauty of the breath too was lost! The heart took over, though in the stillness, it became only too conscious of the scars it bore and its beating itself became a question; the purpose seemed lost… helpless, it urged the other senses to revive, for it was incomplete without them just as all of them were without each other… Each pulled the other and consoled to believe that it's ok to be not ok at times, that it's ok to lose that purpose, that it's ok if the rhythm breaks, it's just really ok…

Gather that indomitable will, gather every piece of you, gather all that you are made of because everything will be ok! Who says the mountain doesn't break? Who says the deepest waters don't have an upheaval? Who says the sky doesn't roar? It's all a journey, it's all a process to be whole, to be you, to be complete. When the clouds hide the sun or the moon, it doesn't mean light wouldn't ever appear. It just means that they are only preparing to shine in their brightest glory. Illuminate from within that no clouds can surmount your light… shine, shine bright that even the darkest nights seem a manifestation of an occasion to brighten up, rise so that even fall seems to fall apart…

Hide and seek was my favorite until upon
my mind and heart started playing it!

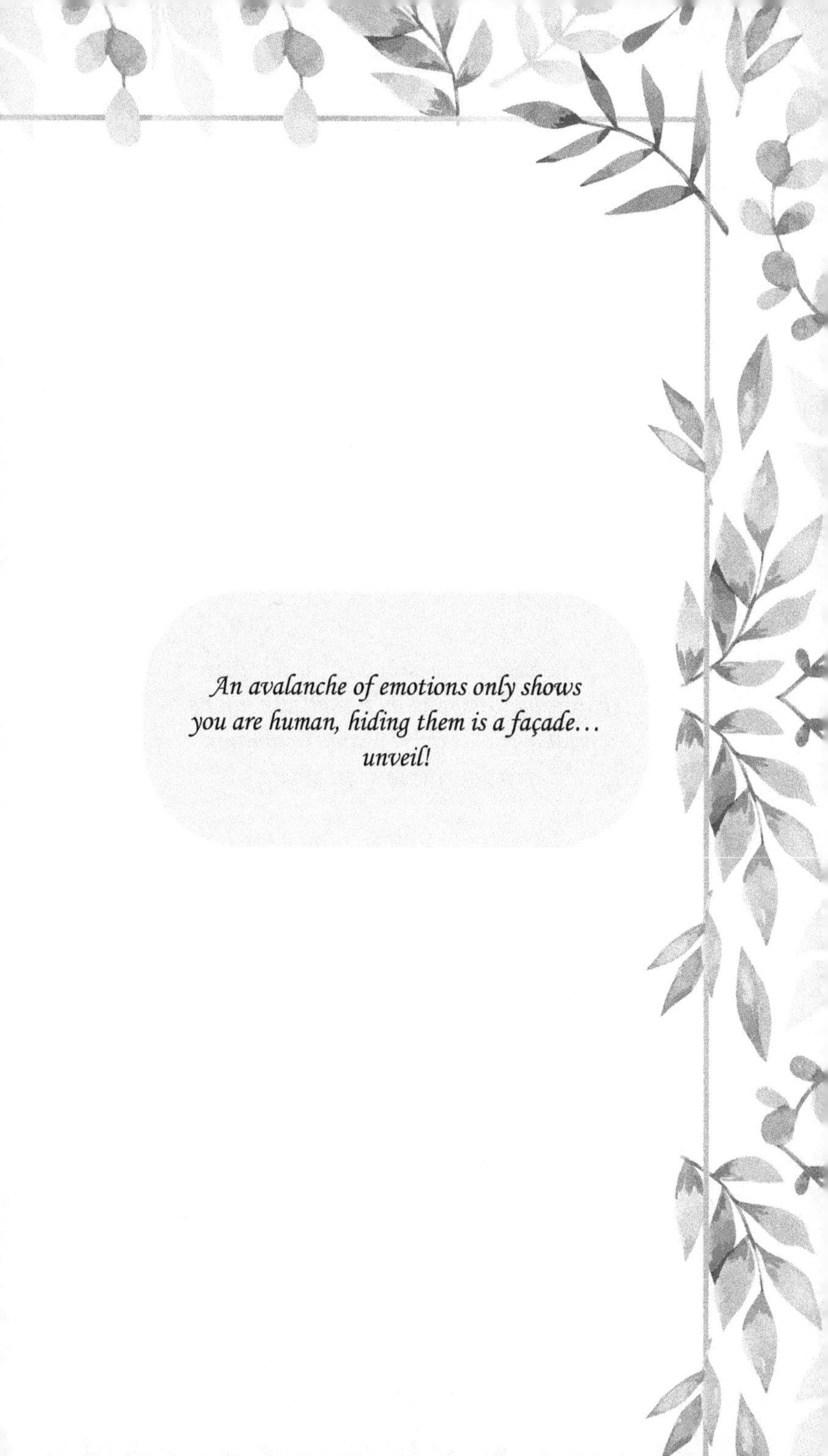

An avalanche of emotions only shows you are human, hiding them is a façade… unveil!

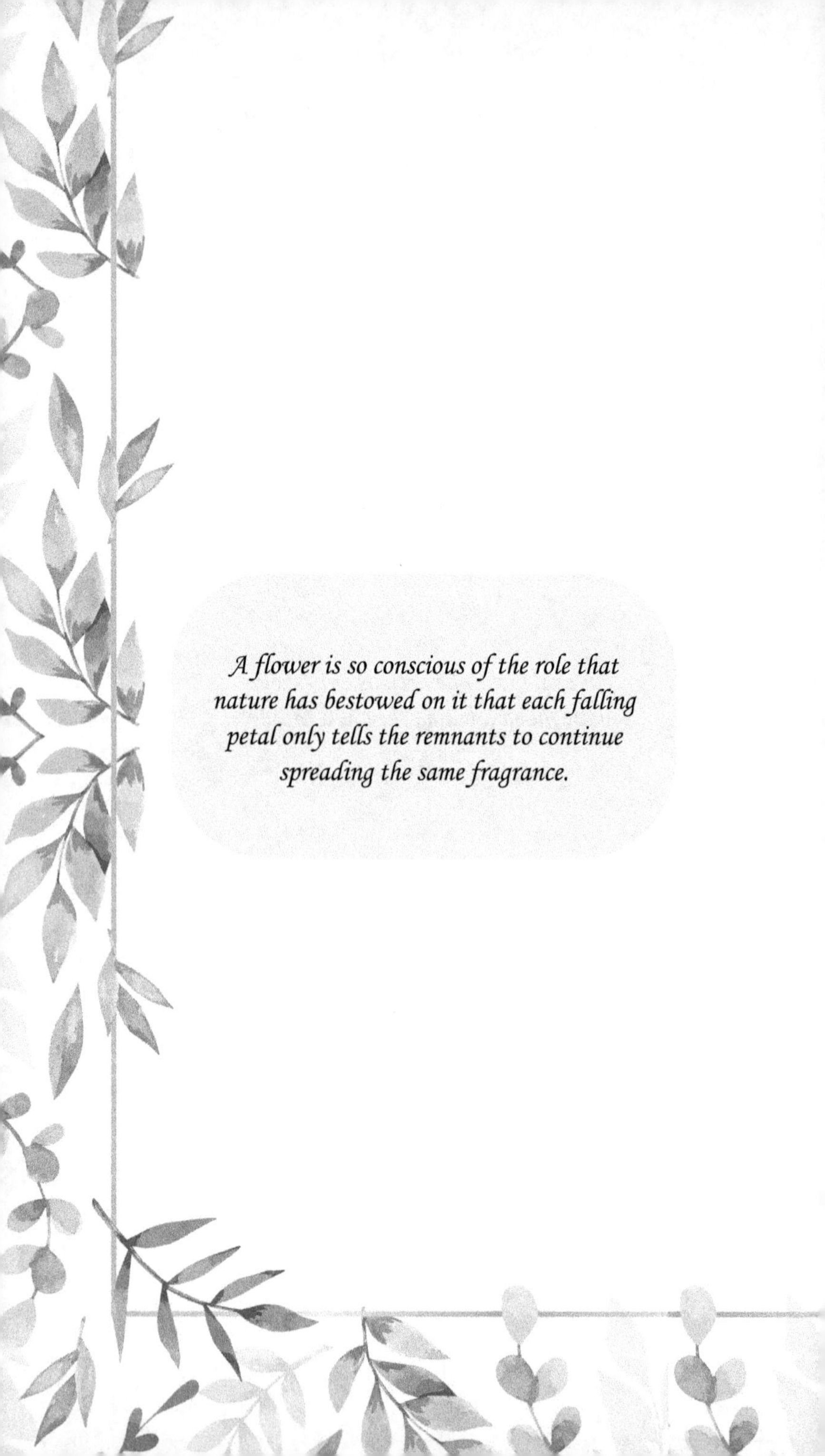

A flower is so conscious of the role that nature has bestowed on it that each falling petal only tells the remnants to continue spreading the same fragrance.

An insight into those dark corners, deep inside, will only help heal… visit them; running away ain't a choice anyway.

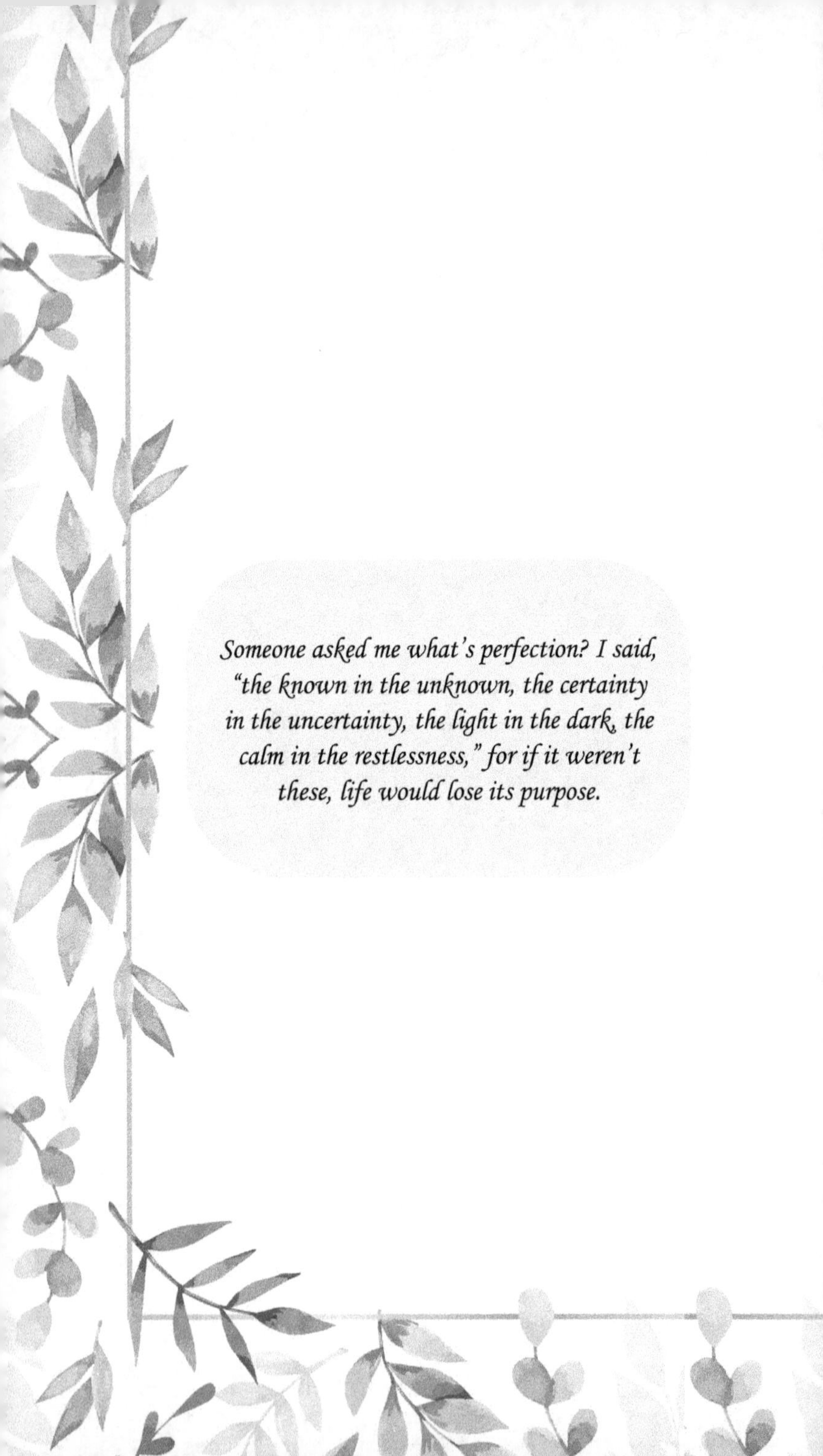

Someone asked me what's perfection? I said, "the known in the unknown, the certainty in the uncertainty, the light in the dark, the calm in the restlessness," for if it weren't these, life would lose its purpose.

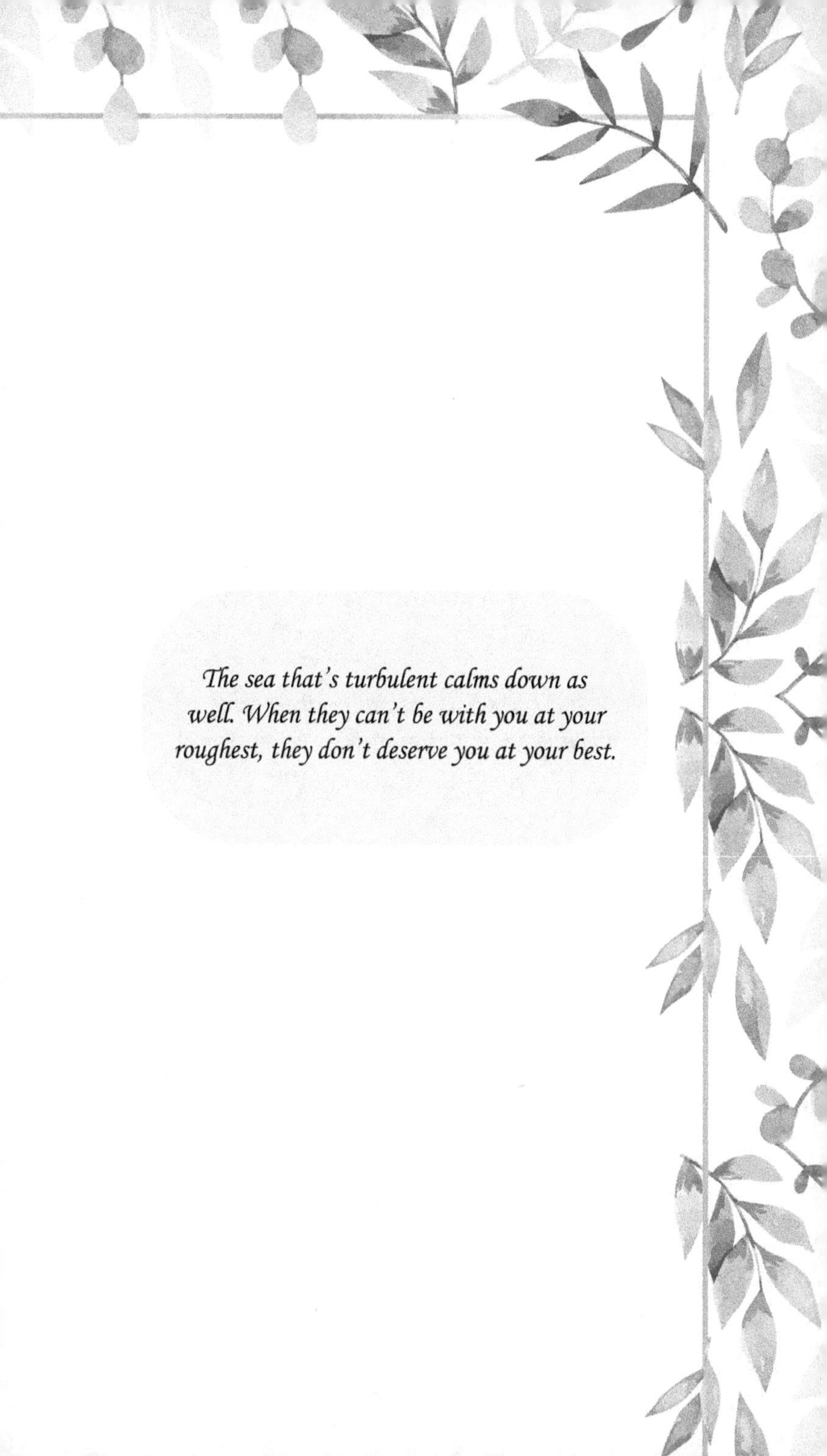

The sea that's turbulent calms down as well. When they can't be with you at your roughest, they don't deserve you at your best.

Darkness is a constant reminder that brightness is incontrovertibly a better choice.

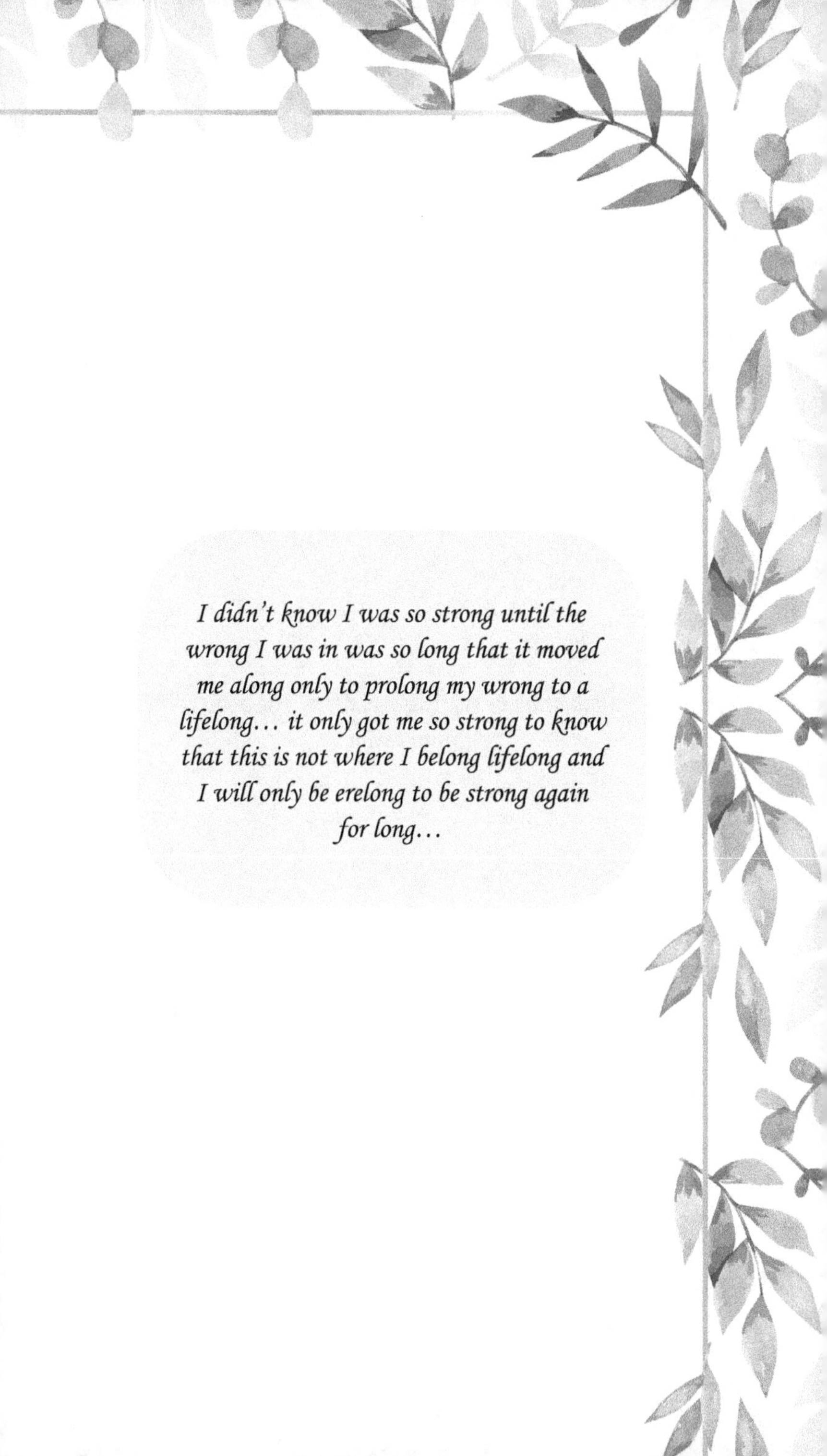

I didn't know I was so strong until the wrong I was in was so long that it moved me along only to prolong my wrong to a lifelong… it only got me so strong to know that this is not where I belong lifelong and I will only be erelong to be strong again for long…

Blame game is a masquerade… rise above;
grow beyond.

It's a misnomer that raised volumes are a symbol of strength; trust, there are no bigger insecurities!

A drop of a tear doesn't mean a fall of a thousand dreams, it only means the eyes shed off what was obstructing the vision of boundless beautiful dreams.

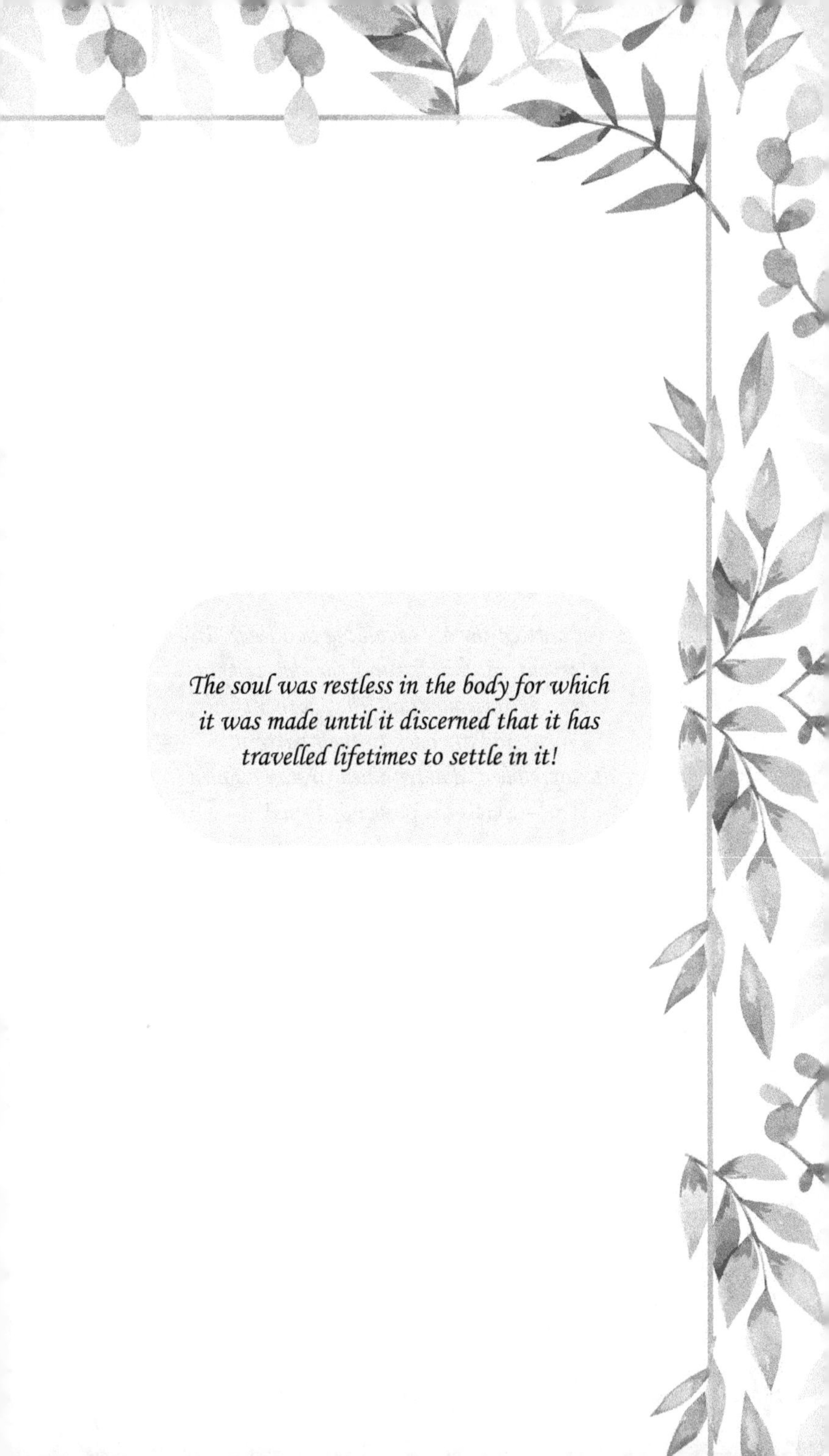

The soul was restless in the body for which it was made until it discerned that it has travelled lifetimes to settle in it!

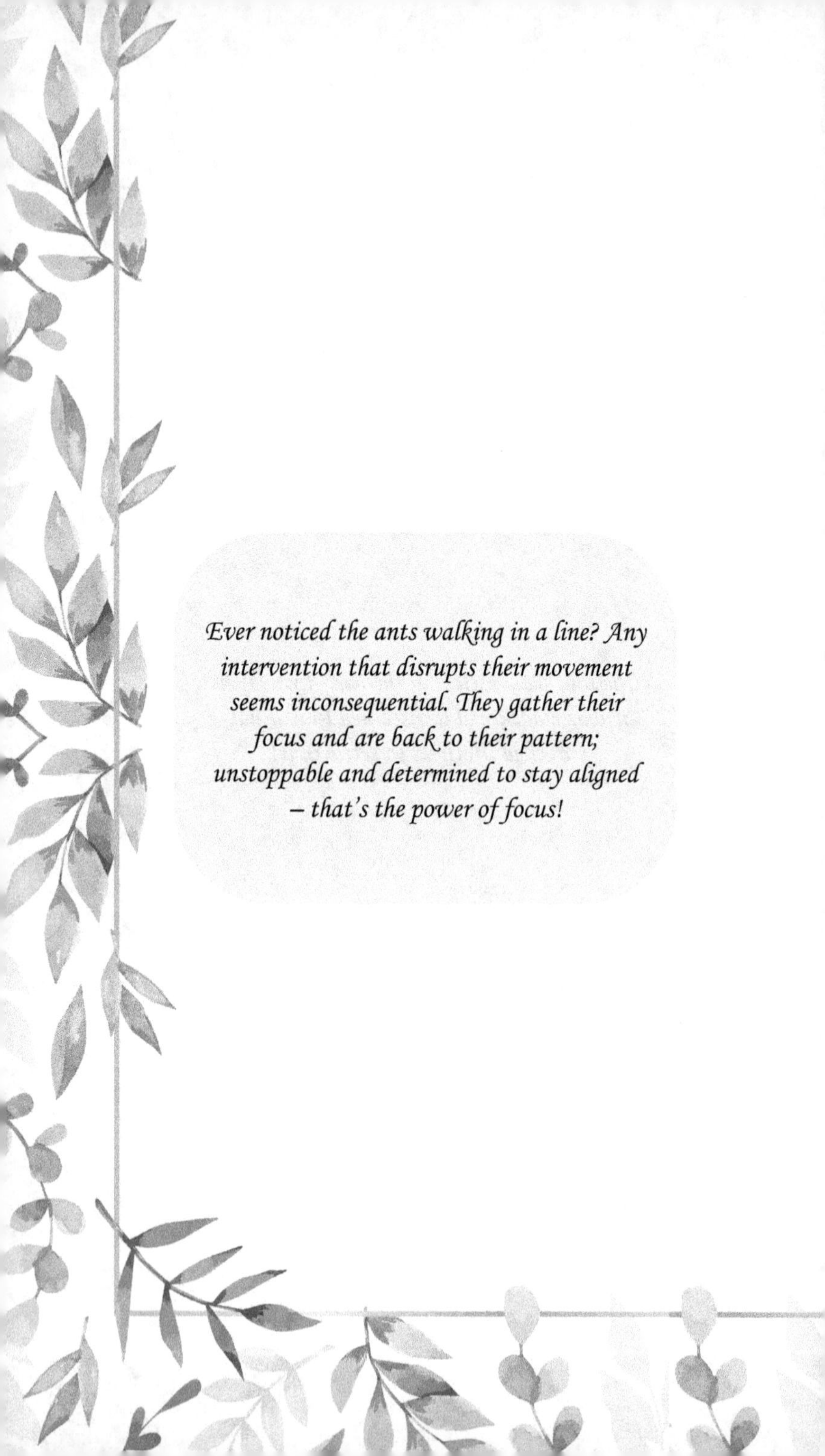

Ever noticed the ants walking in a line? Any intervention that disrupts their movement seems inconsequential. They gather their focus and are back to their pattern; unstoppable and determined to stay aligned – that's the power of focus!

Someone asked me what's being beautiful?
I said, "I inhale and exhale and that's most beautiful." Rejoice!

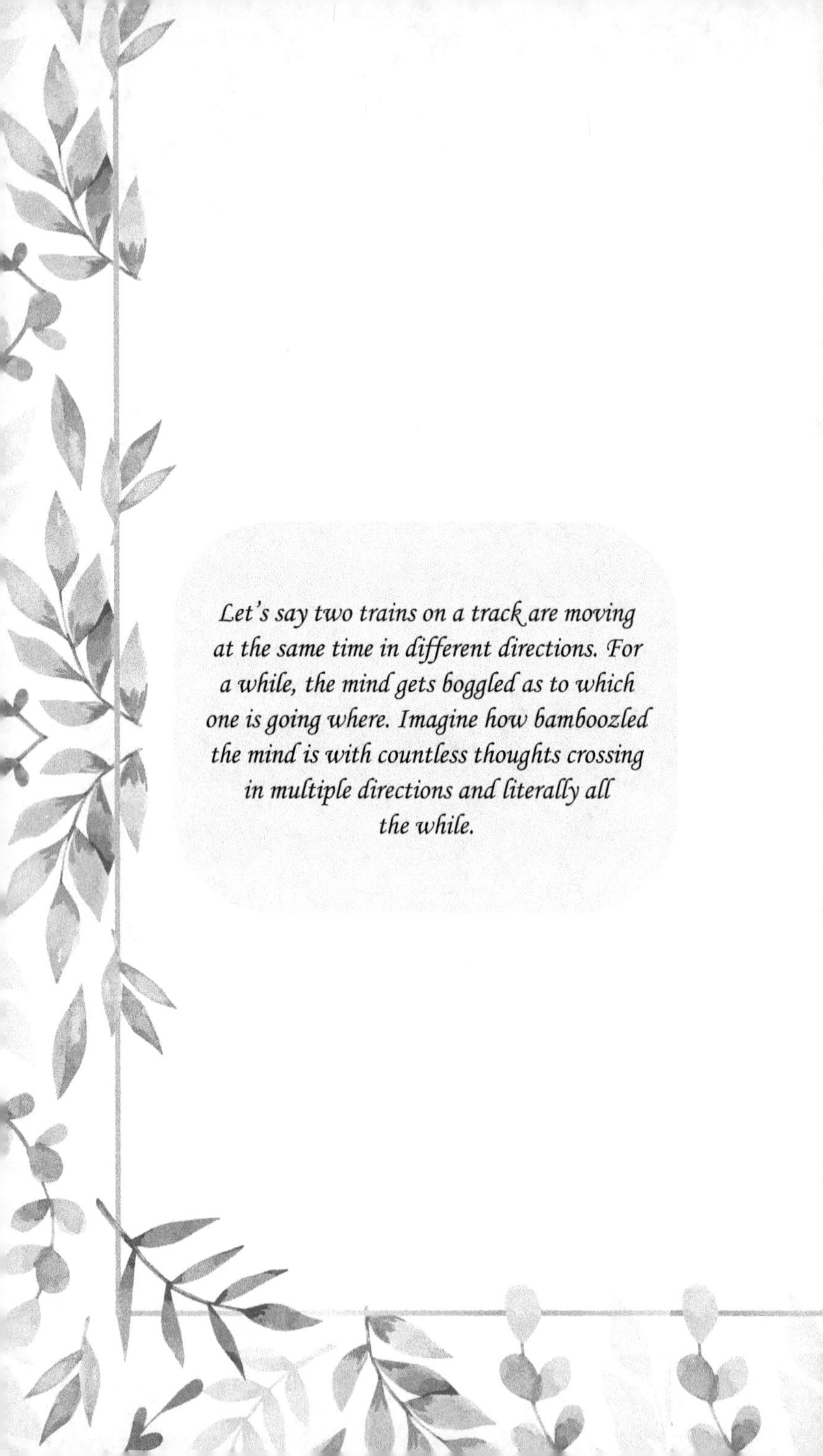

Let's say two trains on a track are moving at the same time in different directions. For a while, the mind gets boggled as to which one is going where. Imagine how bamboozled the mind is with countless thoughts crossing in multiple directions and literally all the while.

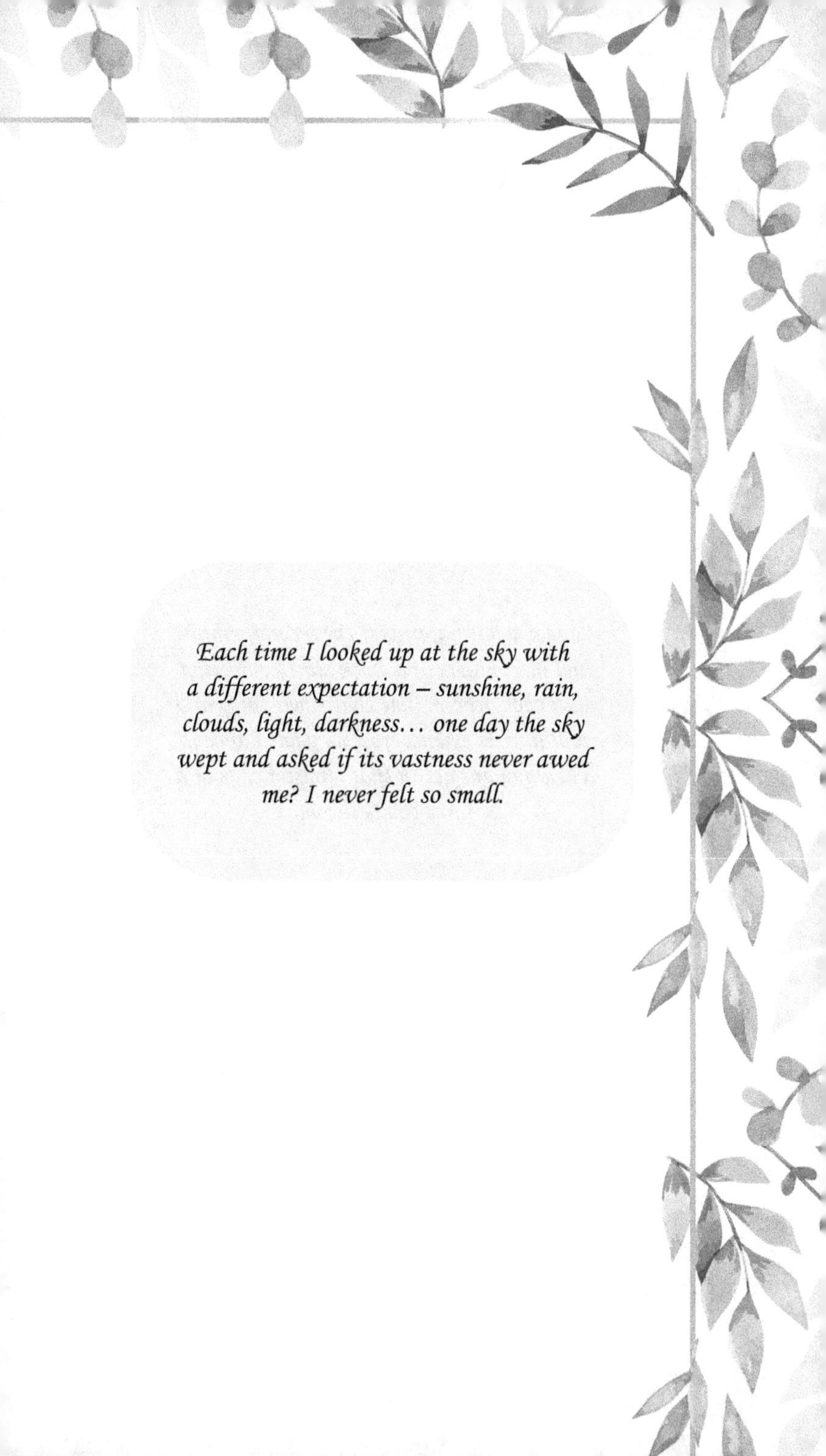

Each time I looked up at the sky with a different expectation – sunshine, rain, clouds, light, darkness… one day the sky wept and asked if its vastness never awed me? I never felt so small.

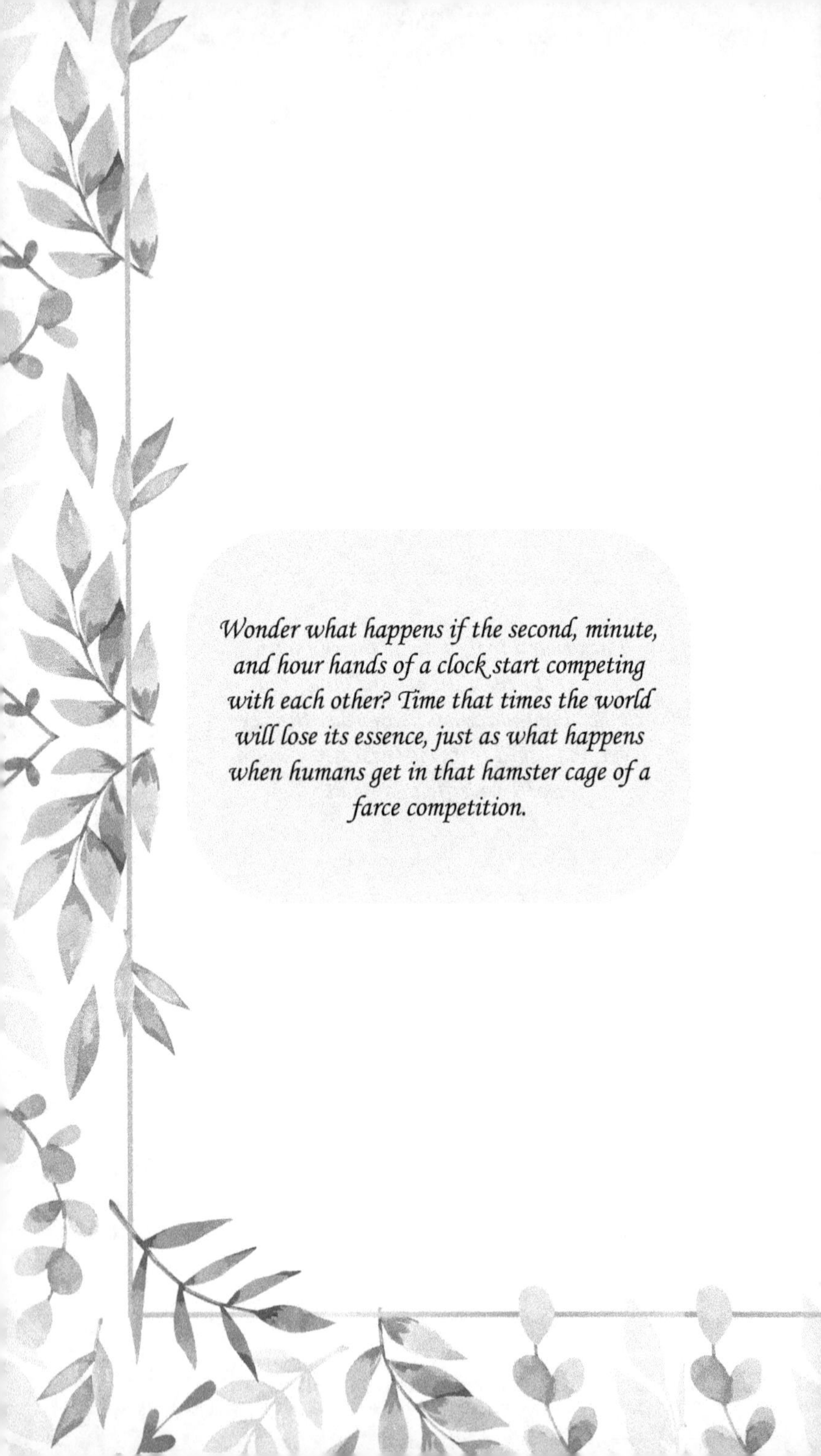

Wonder what happens if the second, minute, and hour hands of a clock start competing with each other? Time that times the world will lose its essence, just as what happens when humans get in that hamster cage of a farce competition.

Accord that irrefutable countenance to be upright, the mountain never needed to justify its solidity.

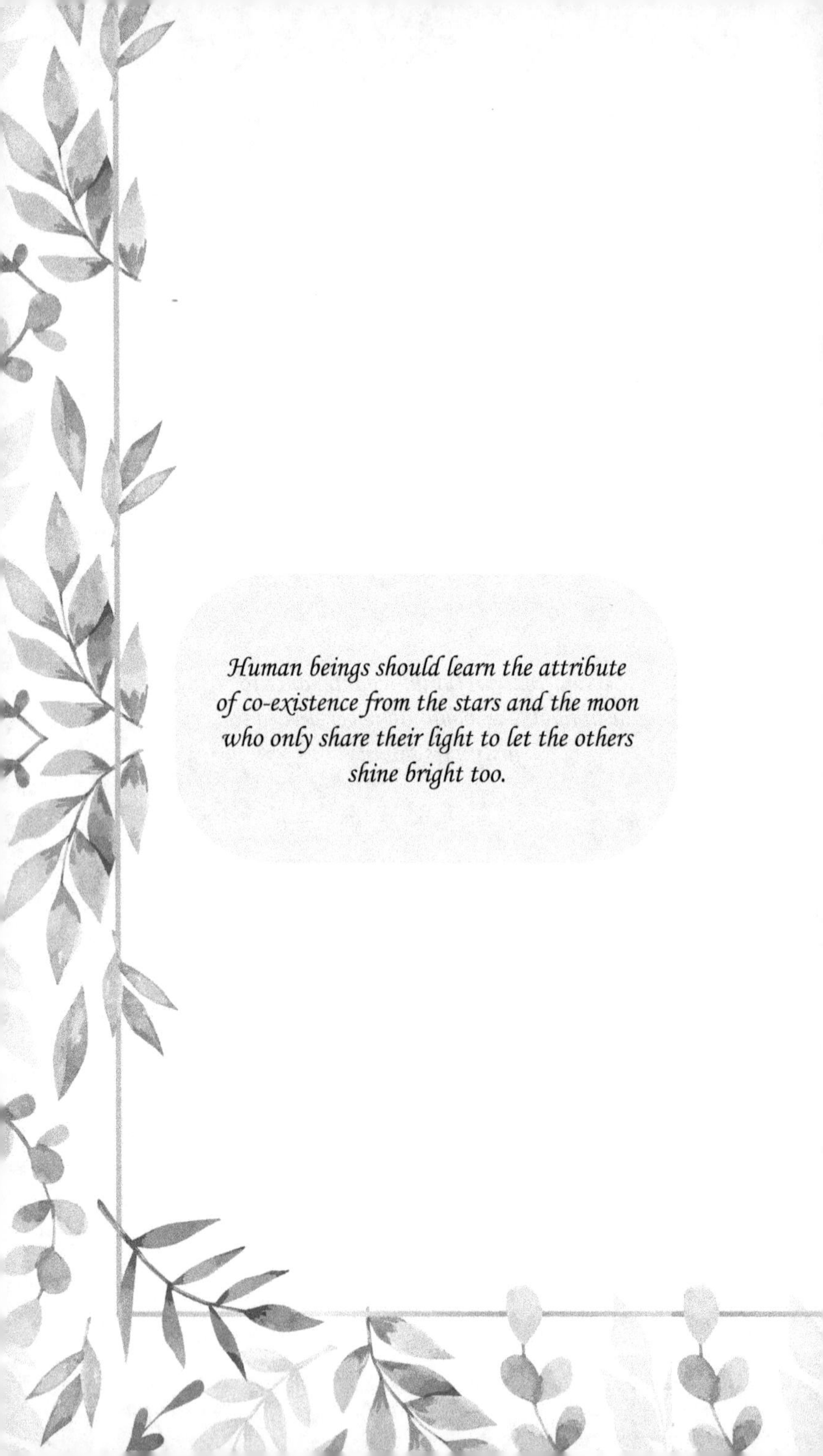

Human beings should learn the attribute of co-existence from the stars and the moon who only share their light to let the others shine bright too.

Just as a flower is as beautiful as the whole bunch, every part of you is as beautiful as the whole you.

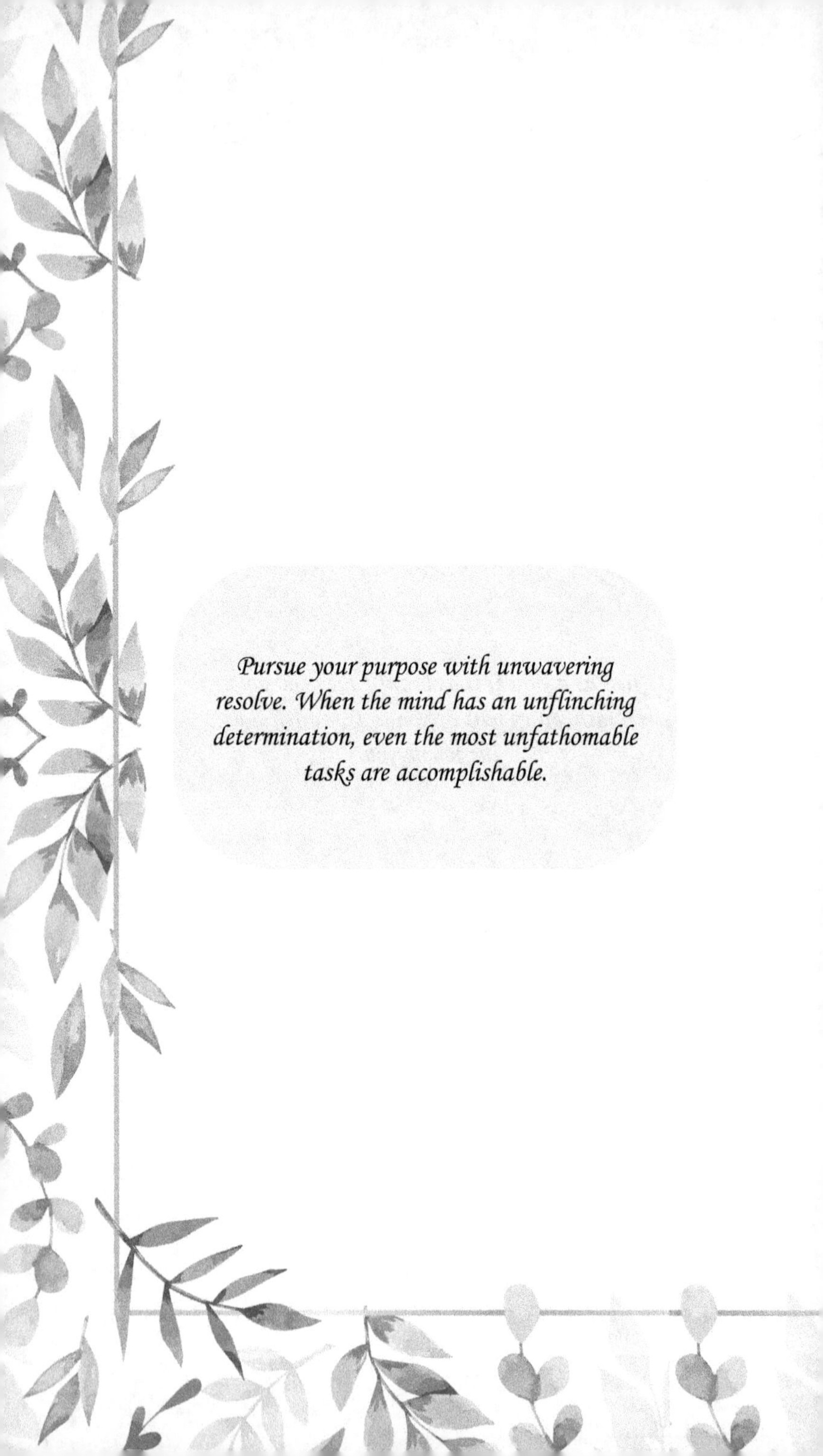

Pursue your purpose with unwavering resolve. When the mind has an unflinching determination, even the most unfathomable tasks are accomplishable.

Pulling the other down is no measure of competition. Rise from within and defeat your own self – you can never be more victorious.

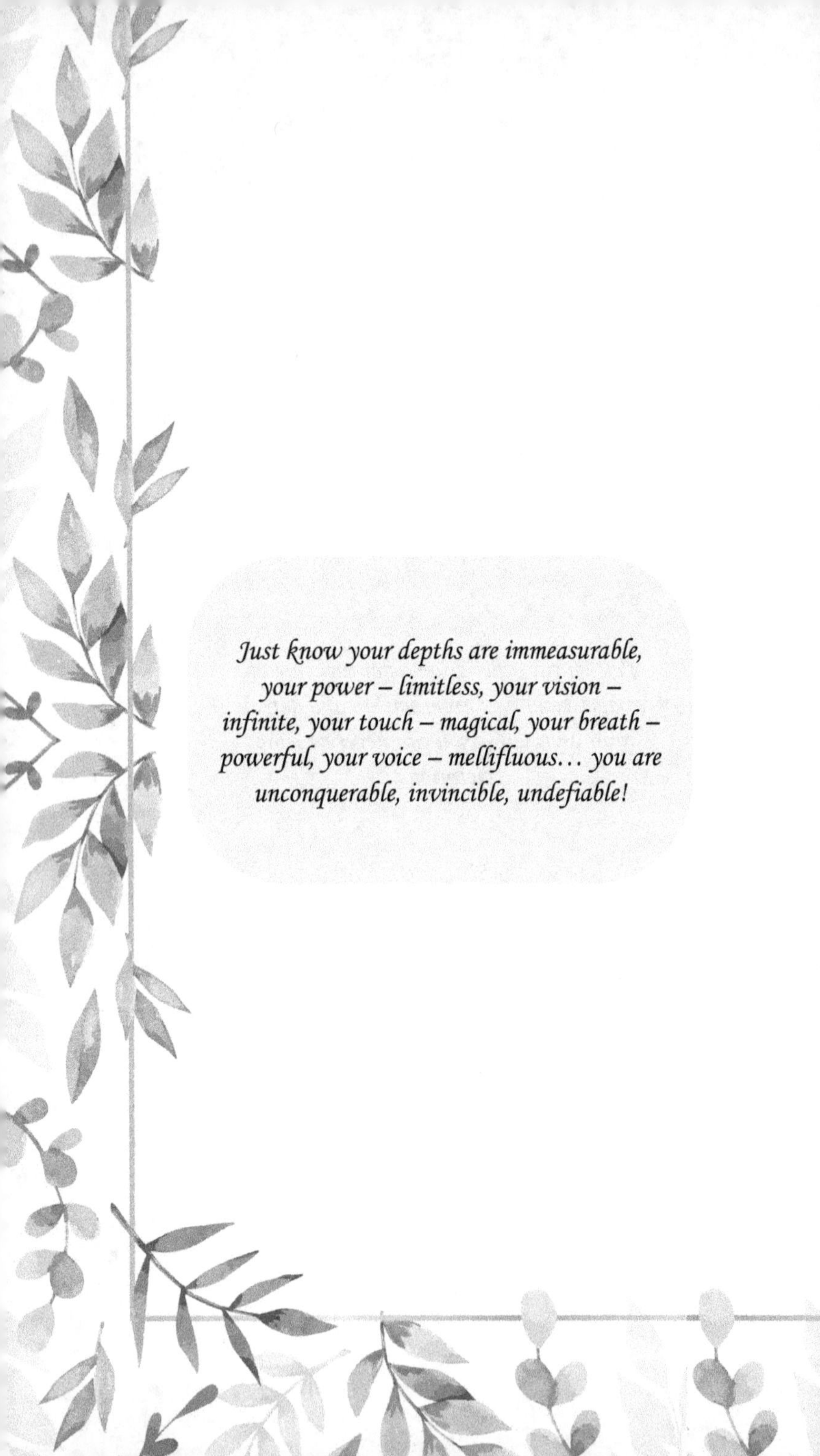

Just know your depths are immeasurable, your power – limitless, your vision – infinite, your touch – magical, your breath – powerful, your voice – mellifluous… you are unconquerable, invincible, undefiable!

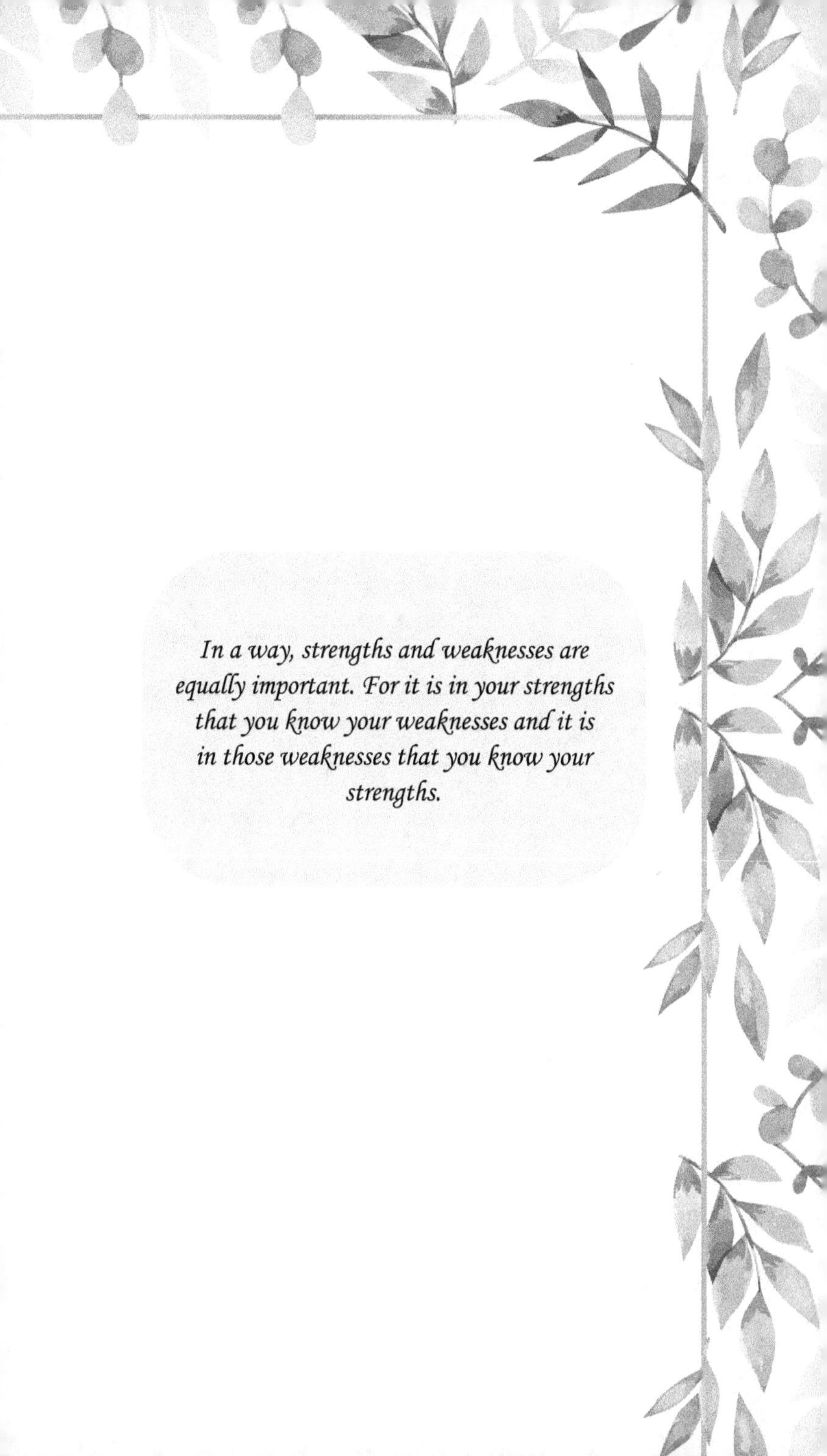

In a way, strengths and weaknesses are equally important. For it is in your strengths that you know your weaknesses and it is in those weaknesses that you know your strengths.

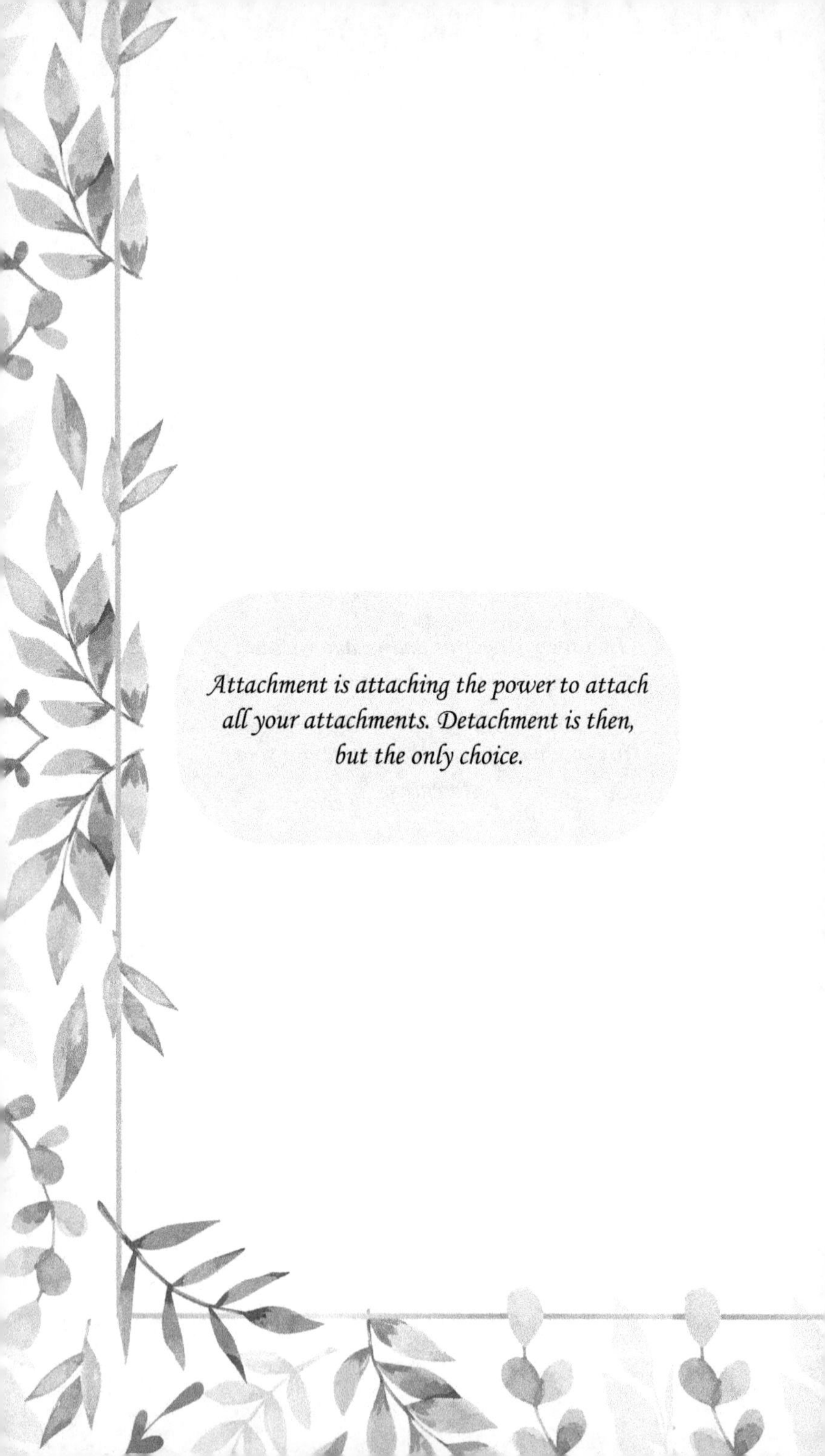

Attachment is attaching the power to attach all your attachments. Detachment is then, but the only choice.

On Role Model:

...Each and every one who has made a difference in my life in any which way at any point in time is my role model. Be it the person whose hand helped me get up when I was shattered under the atrocities of circumstances, or whose words gave me a new ray of hope when I was entrapped in a never-ending darkness, or who showered infinite love that made me feel wanted, or who empowered me to understand the value of adversities! For I believe an individual who has the power to heal someone's life truly deserves to be venerated. The beauty of the soul goes beyond the man-made boundaries of caste, religion, and stature! I thank everyone who chose to live my life with me and touched me with their warmth and love that made me capable enough to be what I am. My thoughts draw to them and my heart itches to give my reverence to them, by being worthy to make a difference in any life that encounters mine!

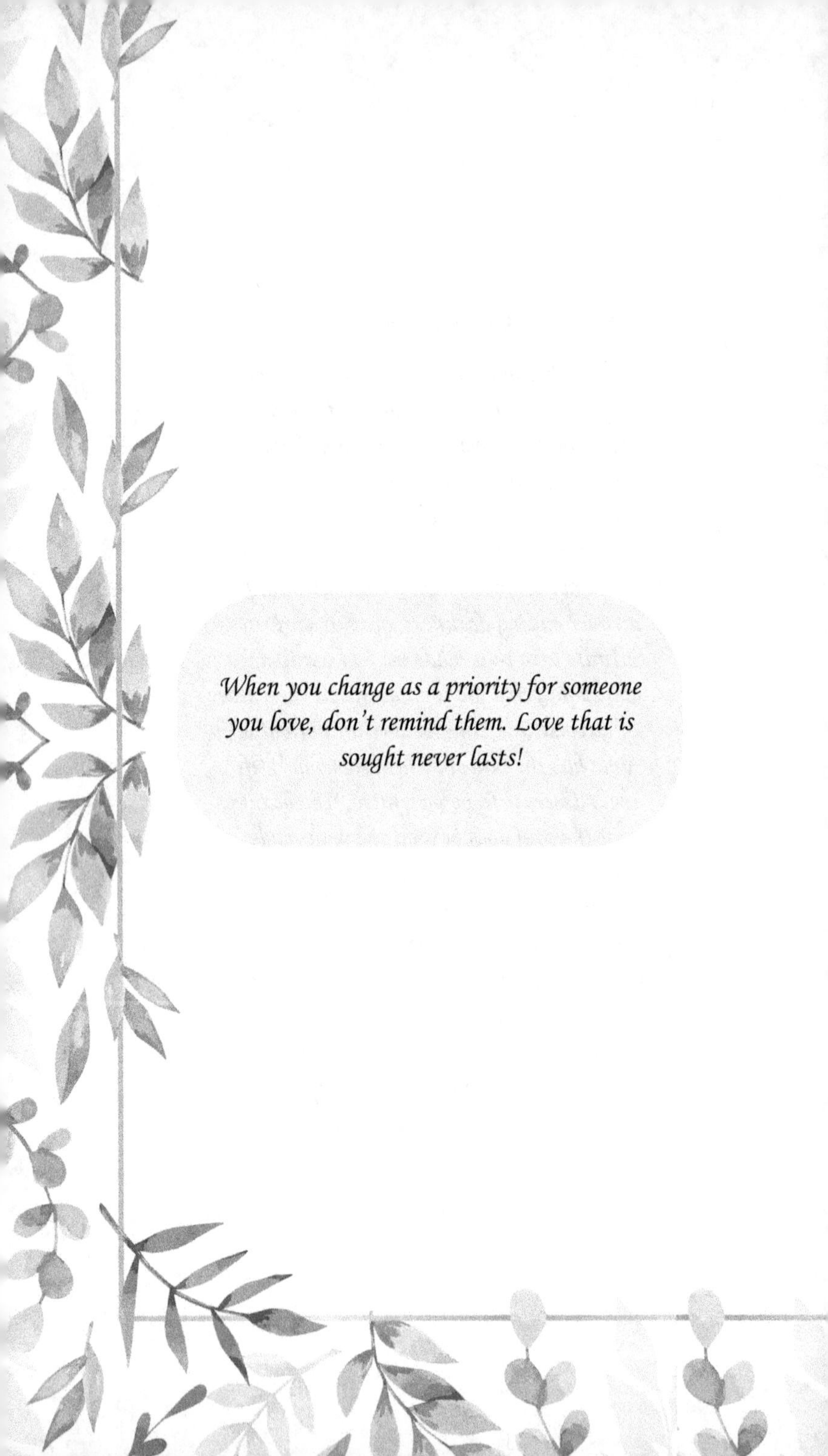

When you change as a priority for someone you love, don't remind them. Love that is sought never lasts!

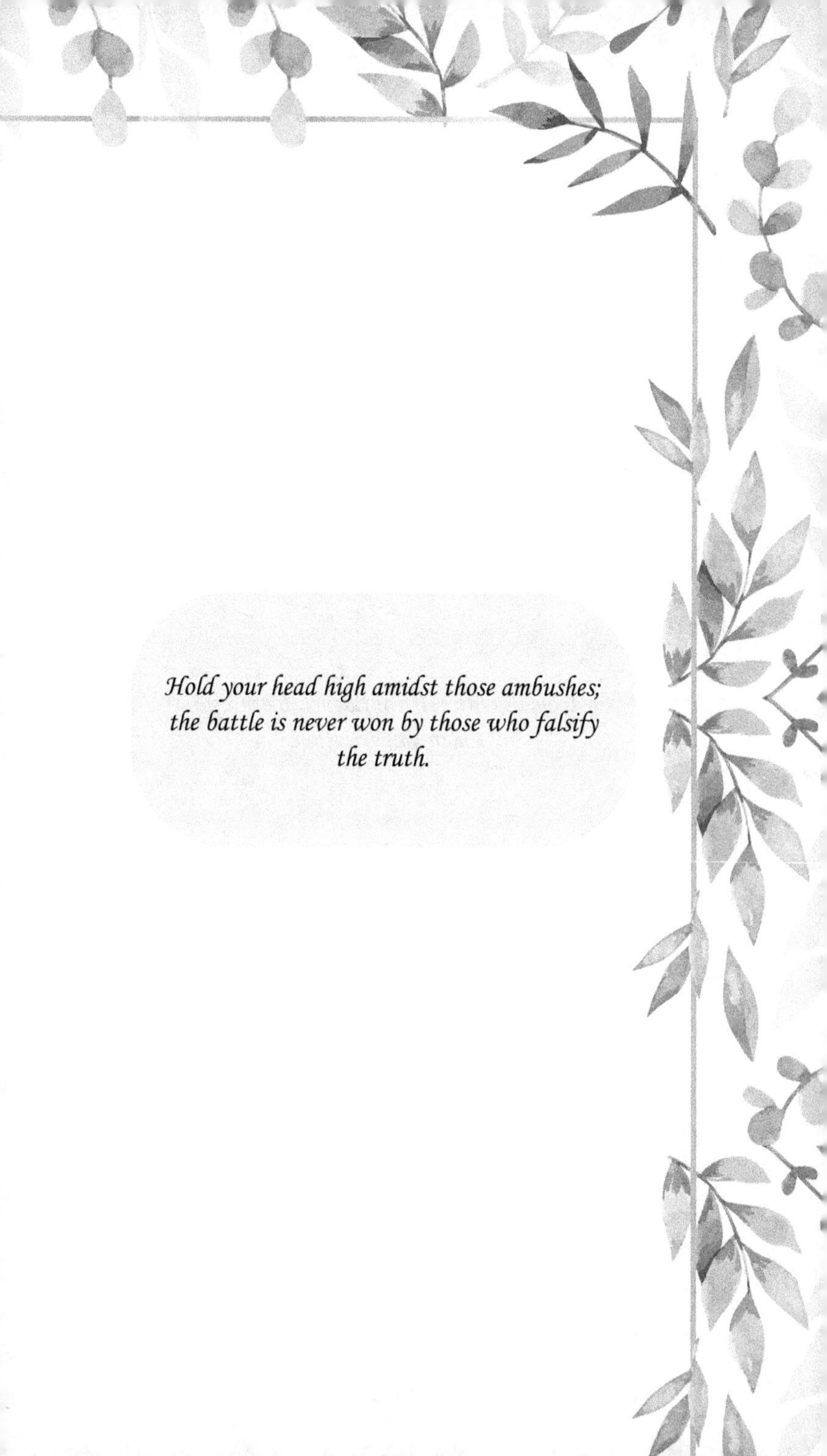

Hold your head high amidst those ambushes; the battle is never won by those who falsify the truth.

A woman with self-confidence doesn't need a man's ratification.

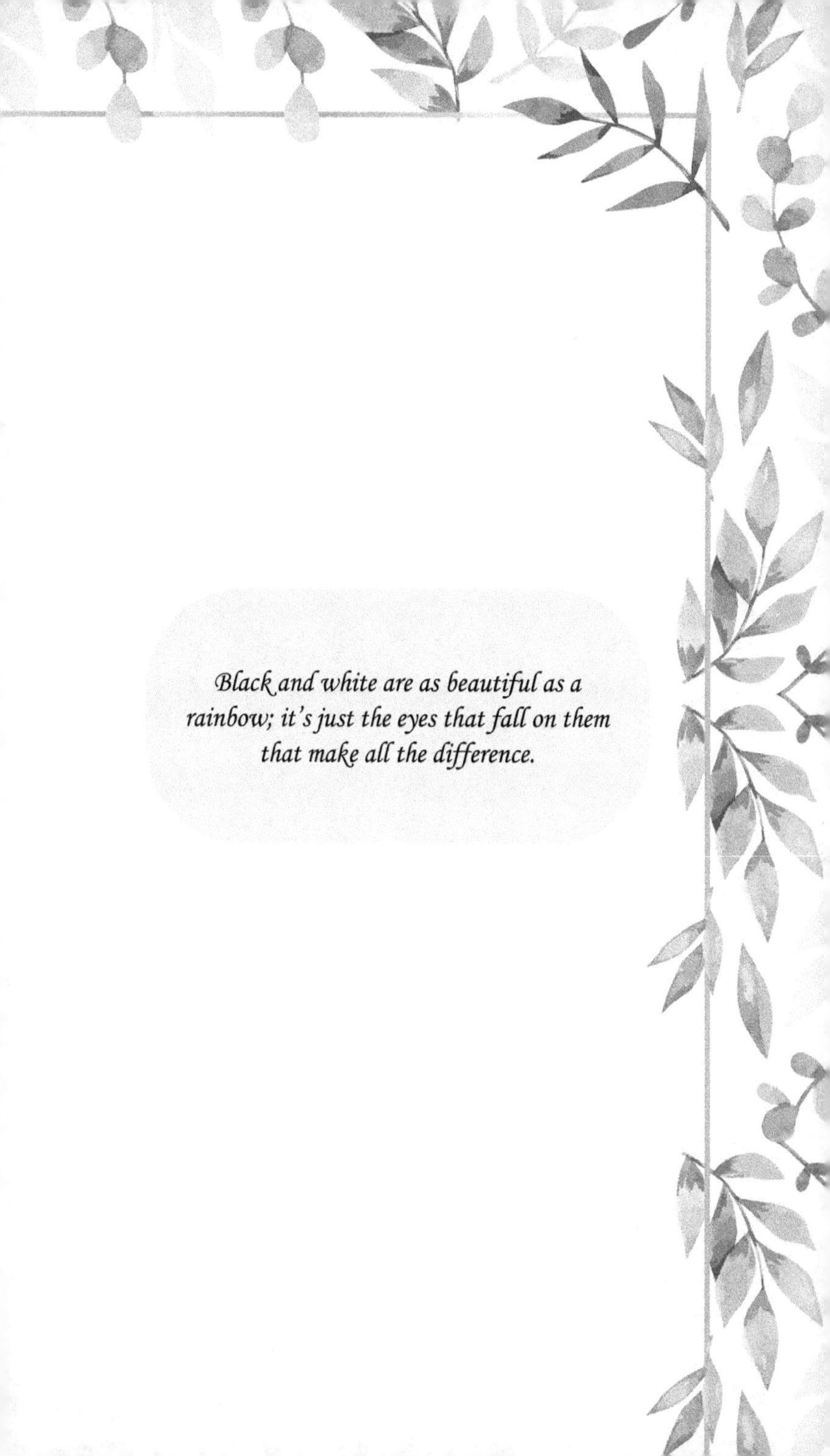

Black and white are as beautiful as a rainbow; it's just the eyes that fall on them that make all the difference.

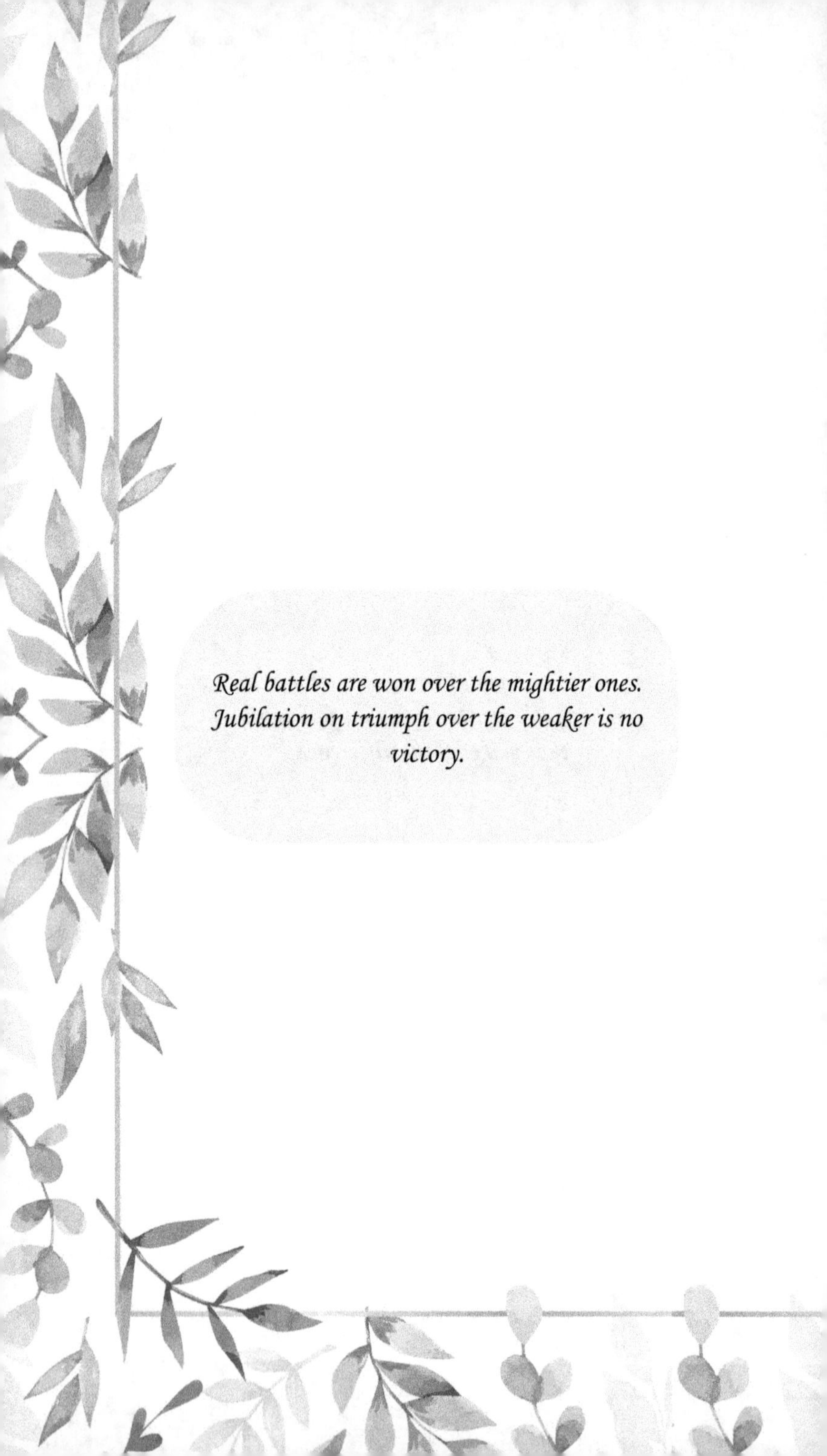

Real battles are won over the mightier ones. Jubilation on triumph over the weaker is no victory.

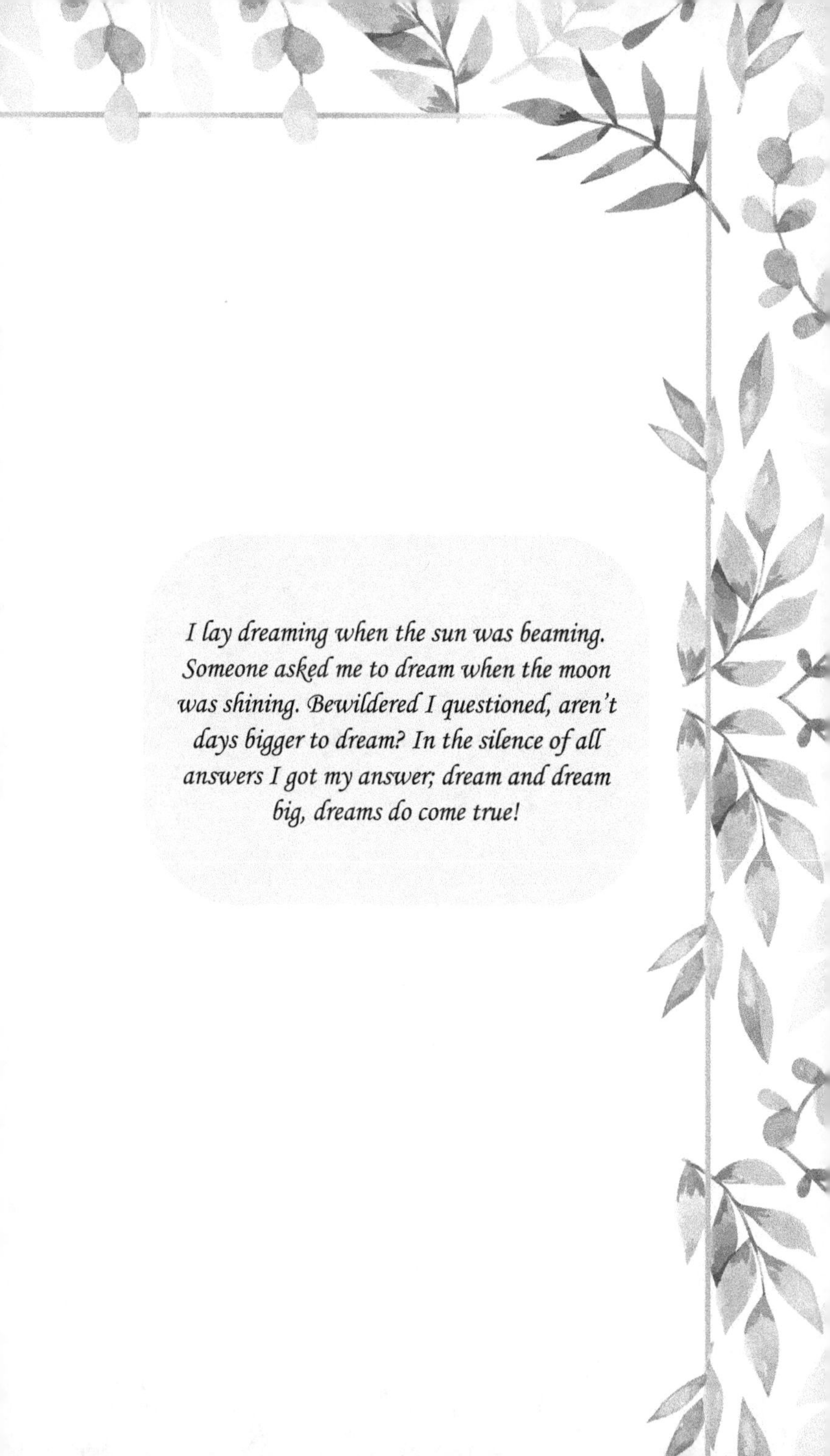

I lay dreaming when the sun was beaming. Someone asked me to dream when the moon was shining. Bewildered I questioned, aren't days bigger to dream? In the silence of all answers I got my answer; dream and dream big, dreams do come true!

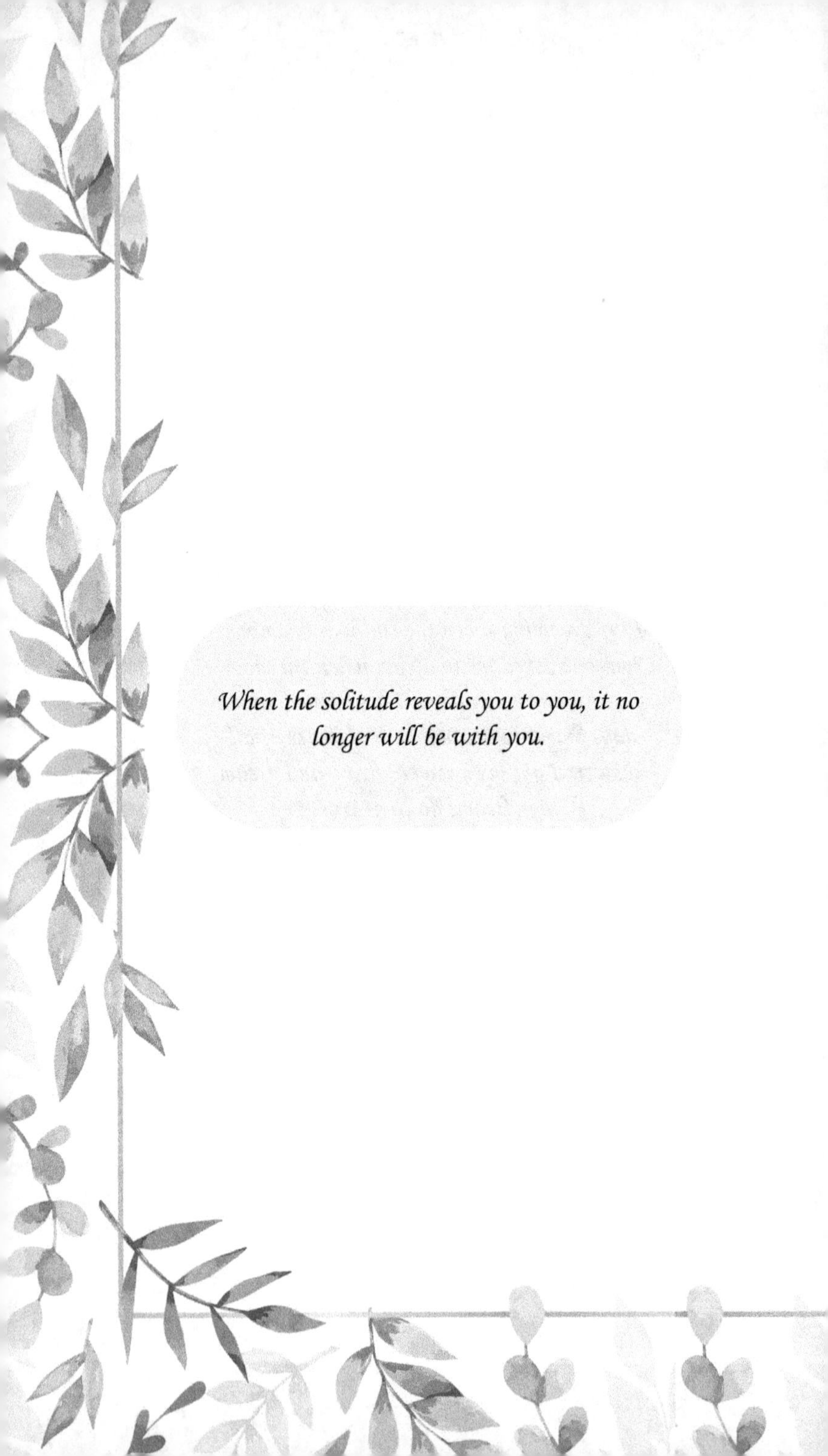

When the solitude reveals you to you, it no longer will be with you.

If a drop can bring such tremors to still water, just imagine the power a thought can bring to a still mind.

Each time you rise like a phoenix… you only emerge to be stronger.

Just as the sky will be at its zenith when the sun and the moon shine together, you are most beautiful in your moments of transition.

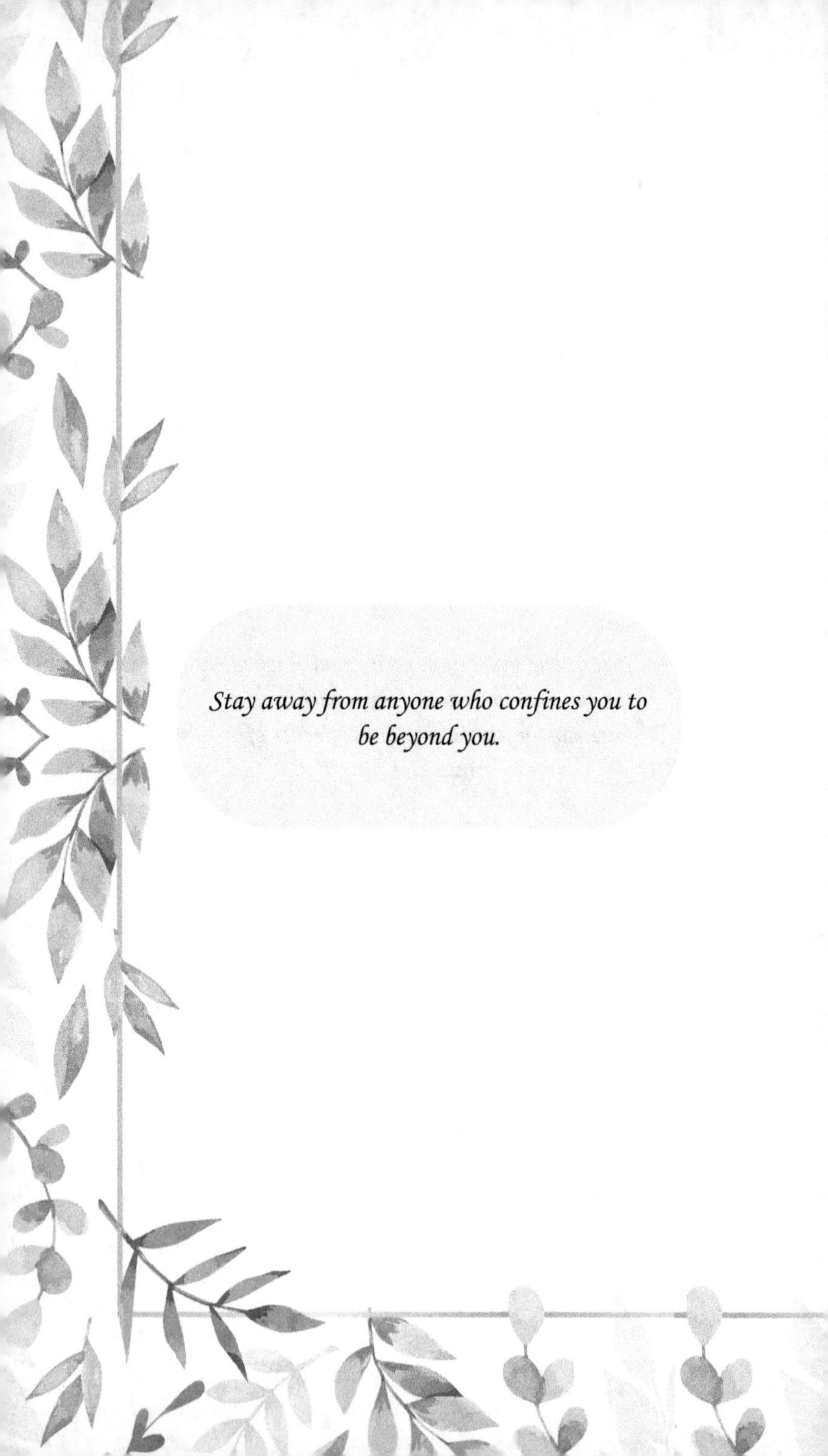

Stay away from anyone who confines you to be beyond you.

Stroke of serendipity is quintessentially a conscious choice.

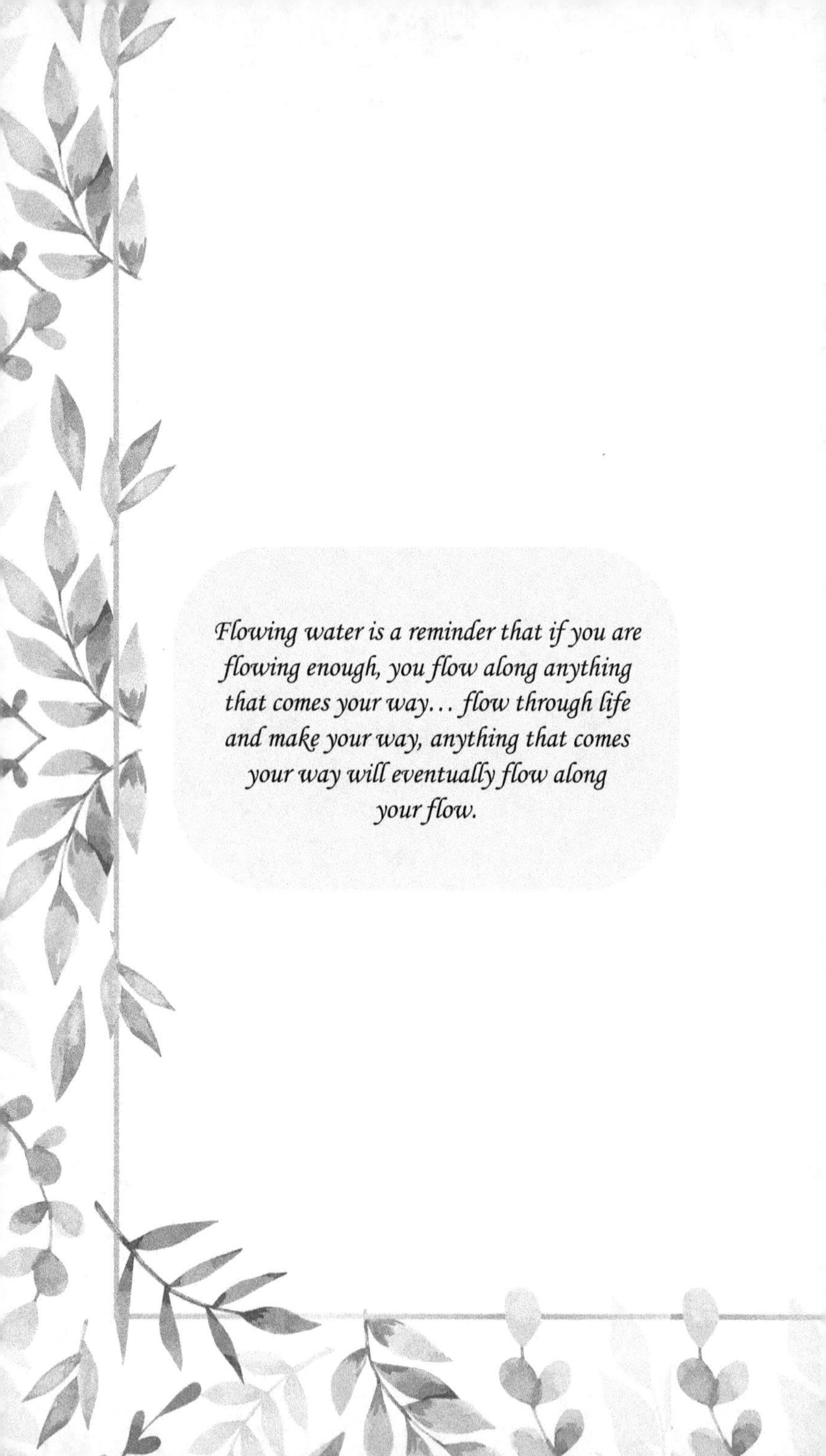

Flowing water is a reminder that if you are flowing enough, you flow along anything that comes your way… flow through life and make your way, anything that comes your way will eventually flow along your flow.

Why always look for a bridge to cross water? Who says sailing through water is any less of a choice?

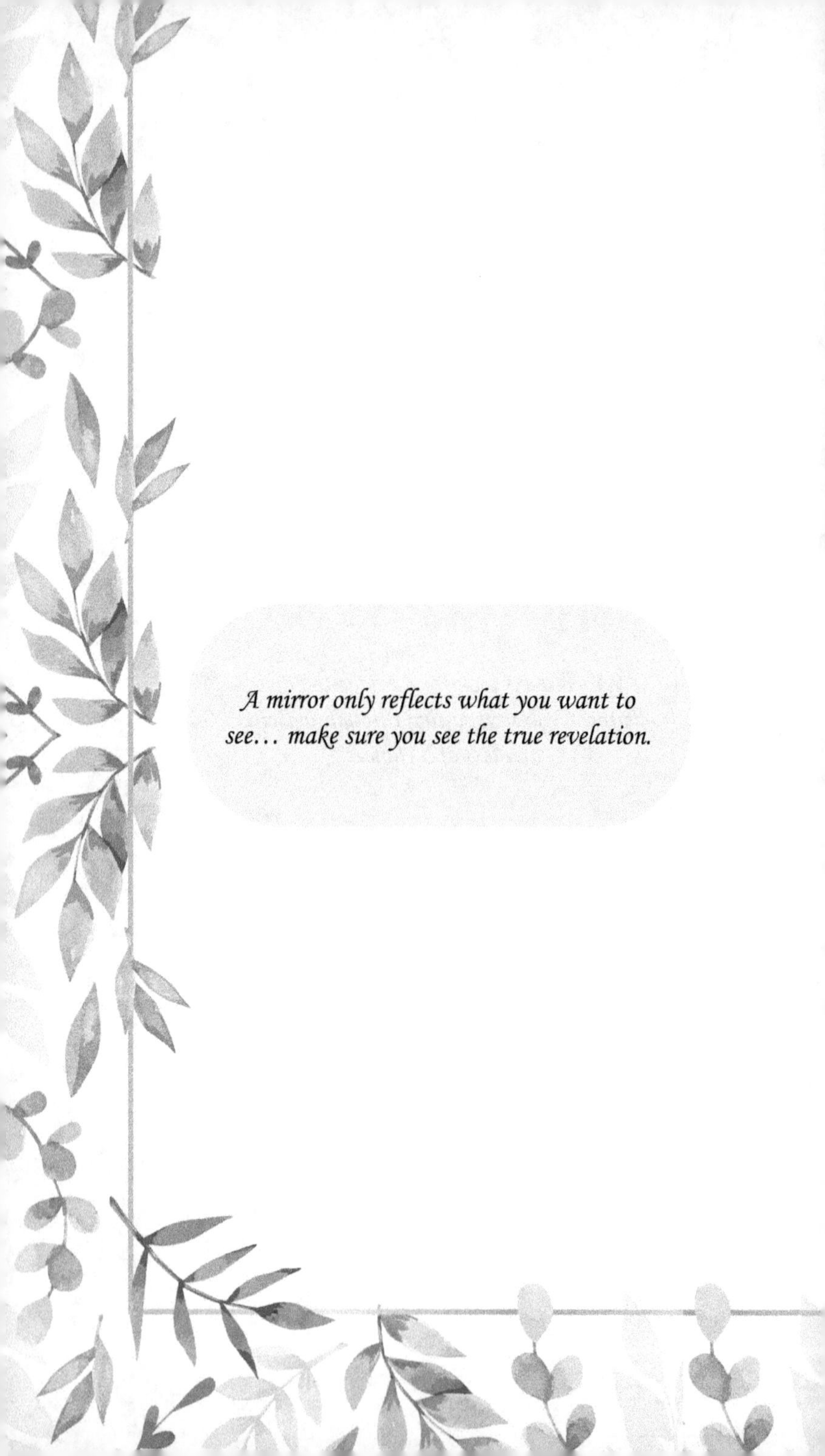

A mirror only reflects what you want to see… make sure you see the true revelation.

When silence becomes your best friend, you both talk louder than words.

You wouldn't say permanence is permanent if you knew the impermanence of even the lines of your hand.

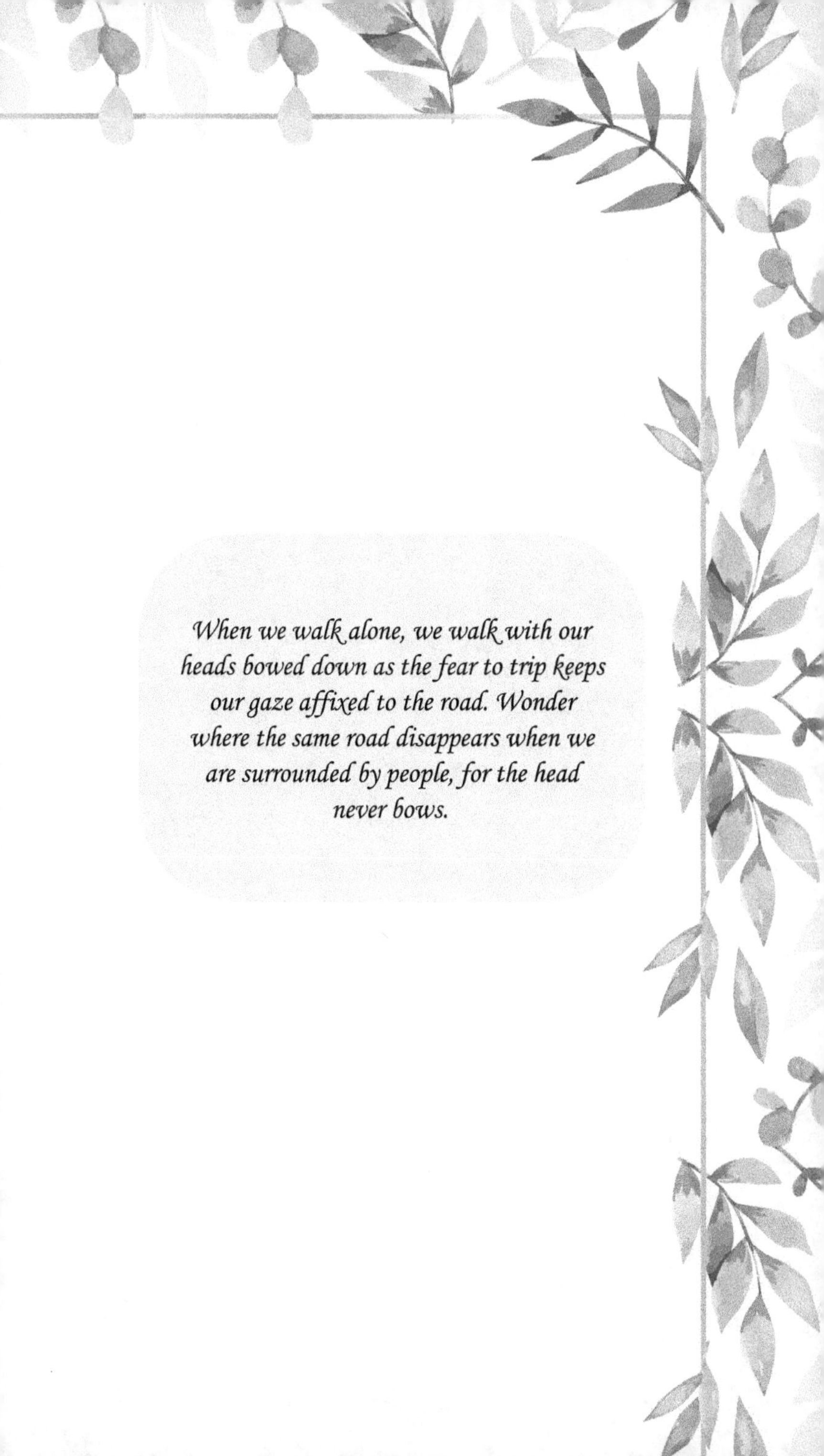

When we walk alone, we walk with our heads bowed down as the fear to trip keeps our gaze affixed to the road. Wonder where the same road disappears when we are surrounded by people, for the head never bows.

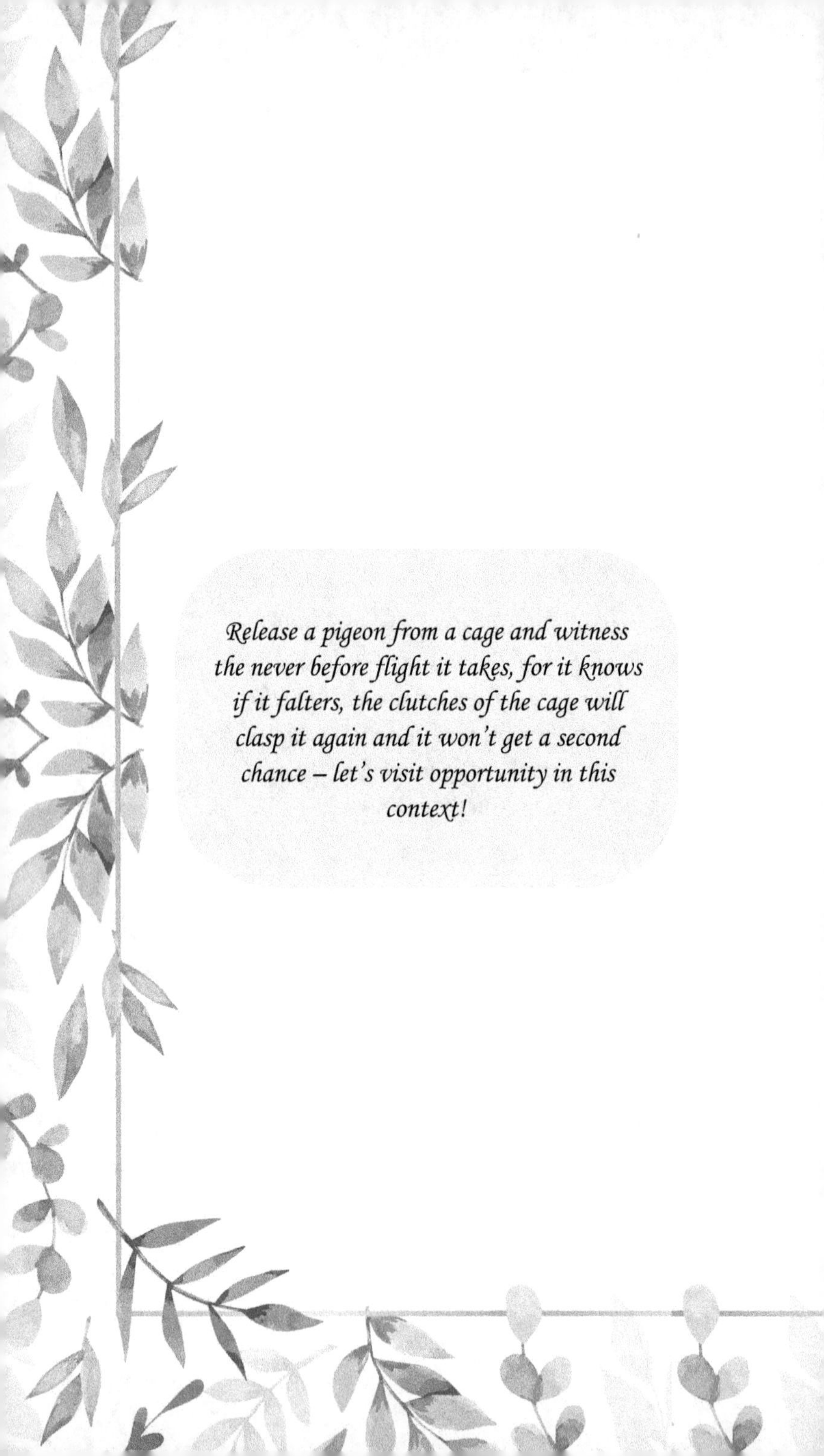

Release a pigeon from a cage and witness the never before flight it takes, for it knows if it falters, the clutches of the cage will clasp it again and it won't get a second chance – let's visit opportunity in this context!

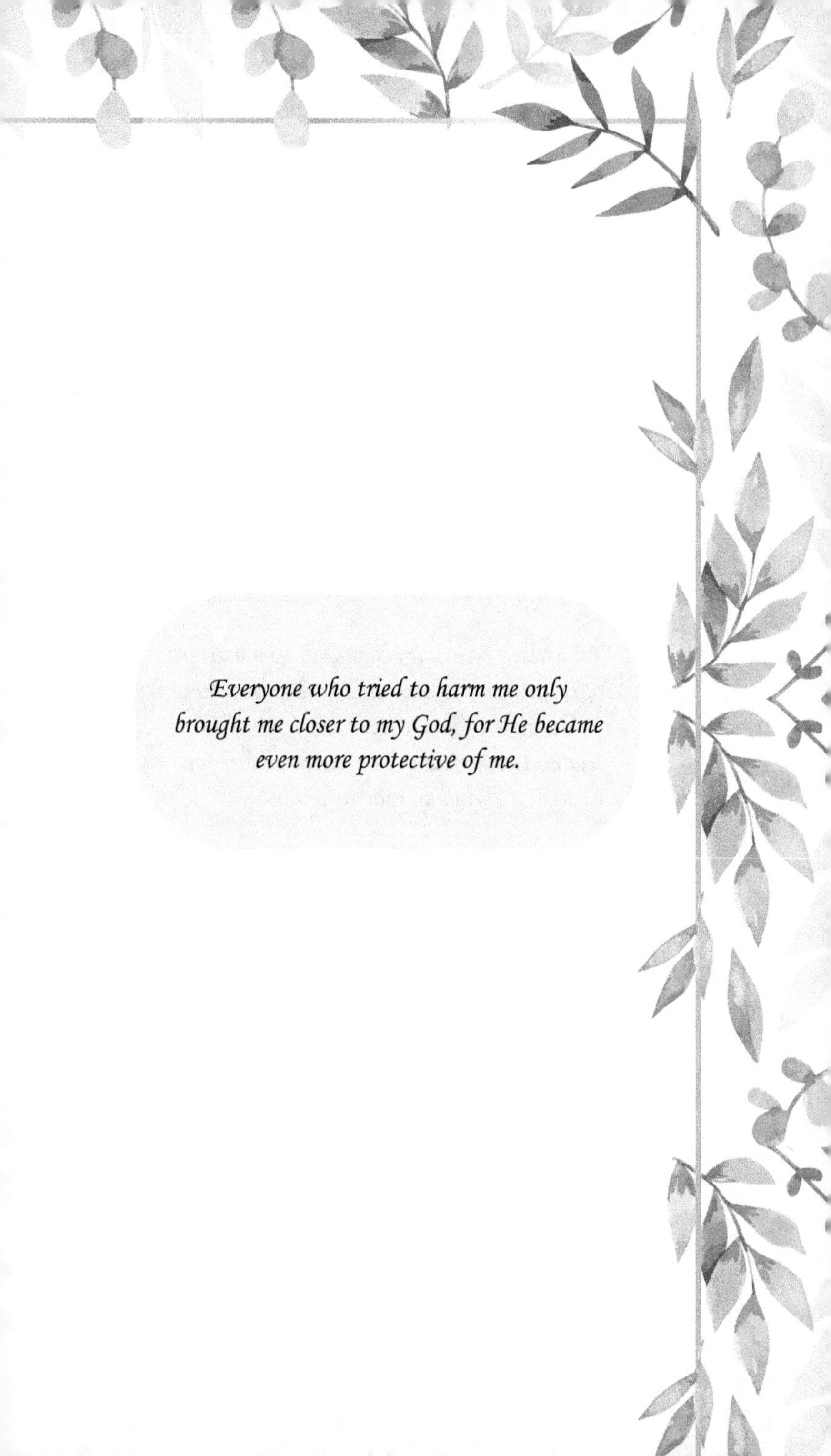

Everyone who tried to harm me only brought me closer to my God, for He became even more protective of me.

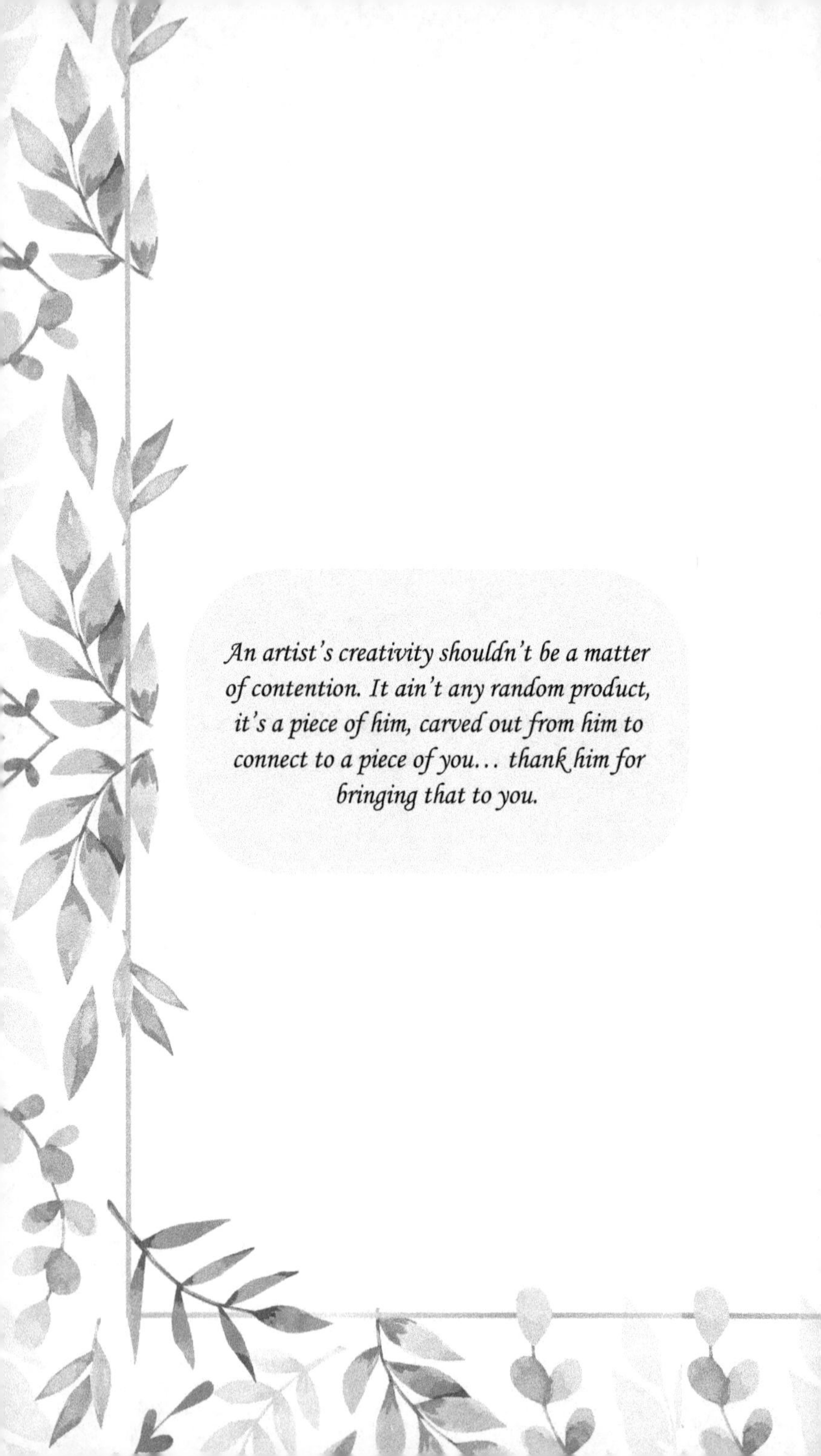

An artist's creativity shouldn't be a matter of contention. It ain't any random product, it's a piece of him, carved out from him to connect to a piece of you... thank him for bringing that to you.

On self-confidence:

A snowflake takes a leap of faith and embarks on a treasurable path by separating from the sky that holds it to have a free fall. It luxuriates in its journey, without the slightest remonstrance that the air is steering its movements; rather, it offers gratitude to the air for driving it to meet the earth where it will become whole. And all along, it dances the most beautiful dance in its esteemed glory for every eye that has the pleasure of witnessing it. It doesn't complain why the sky disowned it or why the earth would absorb it; for it has accepted it as the journey of life… Ain't that a lesson to learn?

Walk away from those who seek justification in you being YOU!

Childhood to adulthood only changed my smile from innocence to artificial; wonder what I have been through…

Life is beautiful or beautiful is life – the assurance is only a matter of a changed perspective! Think about it!

Confidence gives a woman an unsurpassed sex appeal! Stay strong; stay beautiful!

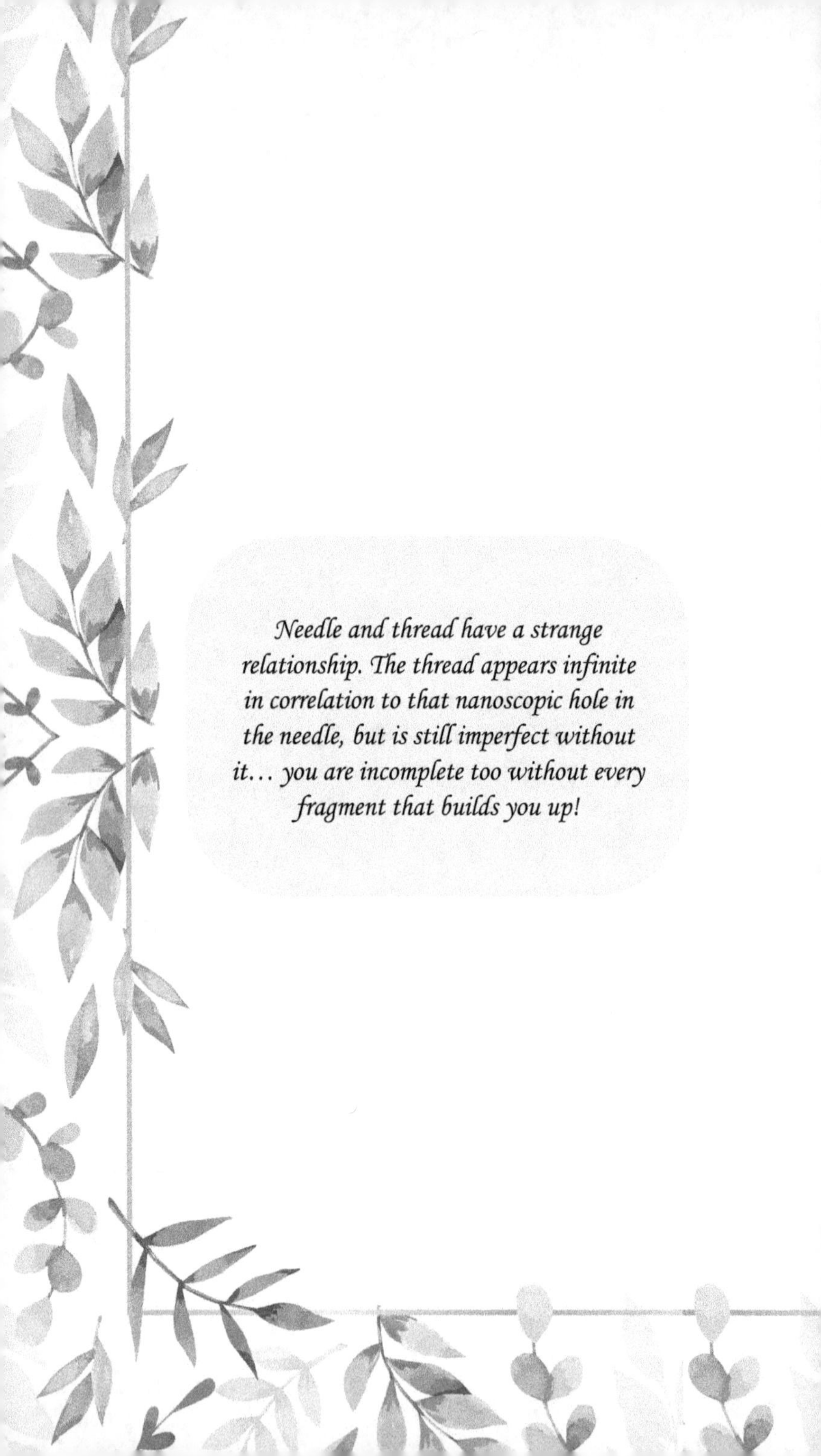

Needle and thread have a strange relationship. The thread appears infinite in correlation to that nanoscopic hole in the needle, but is still imperfect without it… you are incomplete too without every fragment that builds you up!

A hand to uplift someone up only helps you heal a part of yourself. Add meaning; be meaningful!

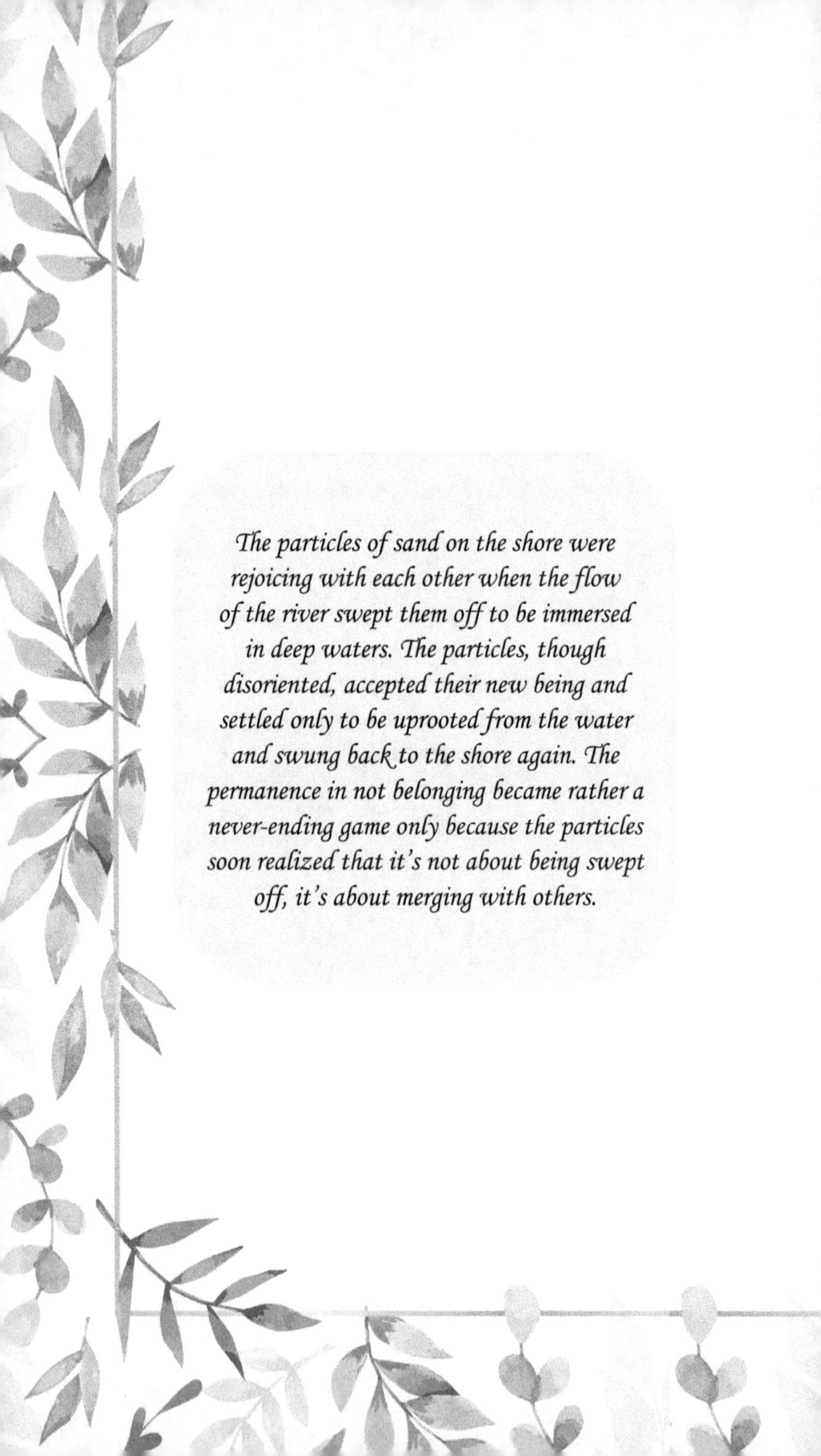

The particles of sand on the shore were rejoicing with each other when the flow of the river swept them off to be immersed in deep waters. The particles, though disoriented, accepted their new being and settled only to be uprooted from the water and swung back to the shore again. The permanence in not belonging became rather a never-ending game only because the particles soon realized that it's not about being swept off, it's about merging with others.

A pre-scripted dimension to life will only make it nondescript. Wander and explore, for the thrill will be unbeatable.

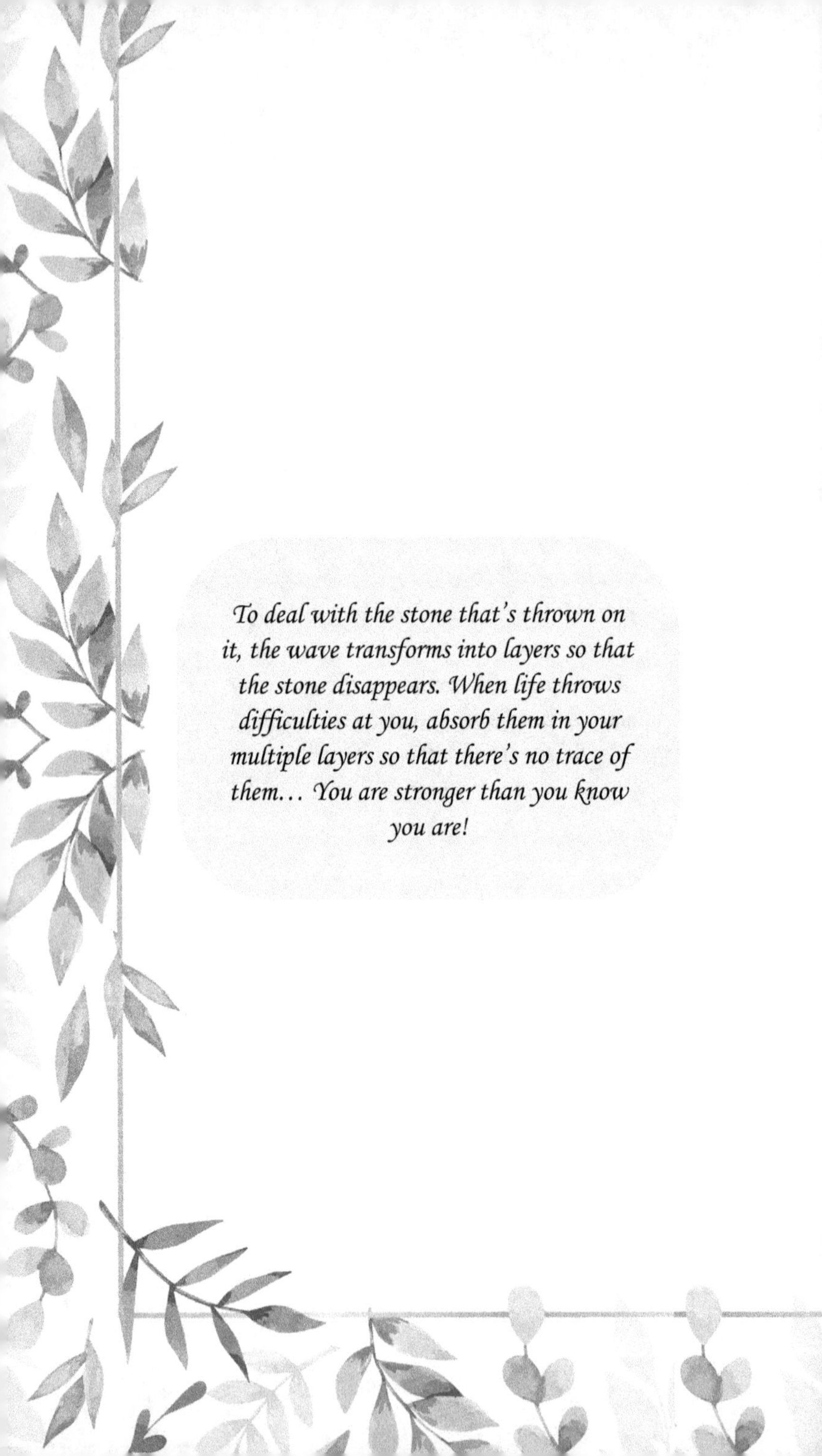

To deal with the stone that's thrown on it, the wave transforms into layers so that the stone disappears. When life throws difficulties at you, absorb them in your multiple layers so that there's no trace of them… You are stronger than you know you are!

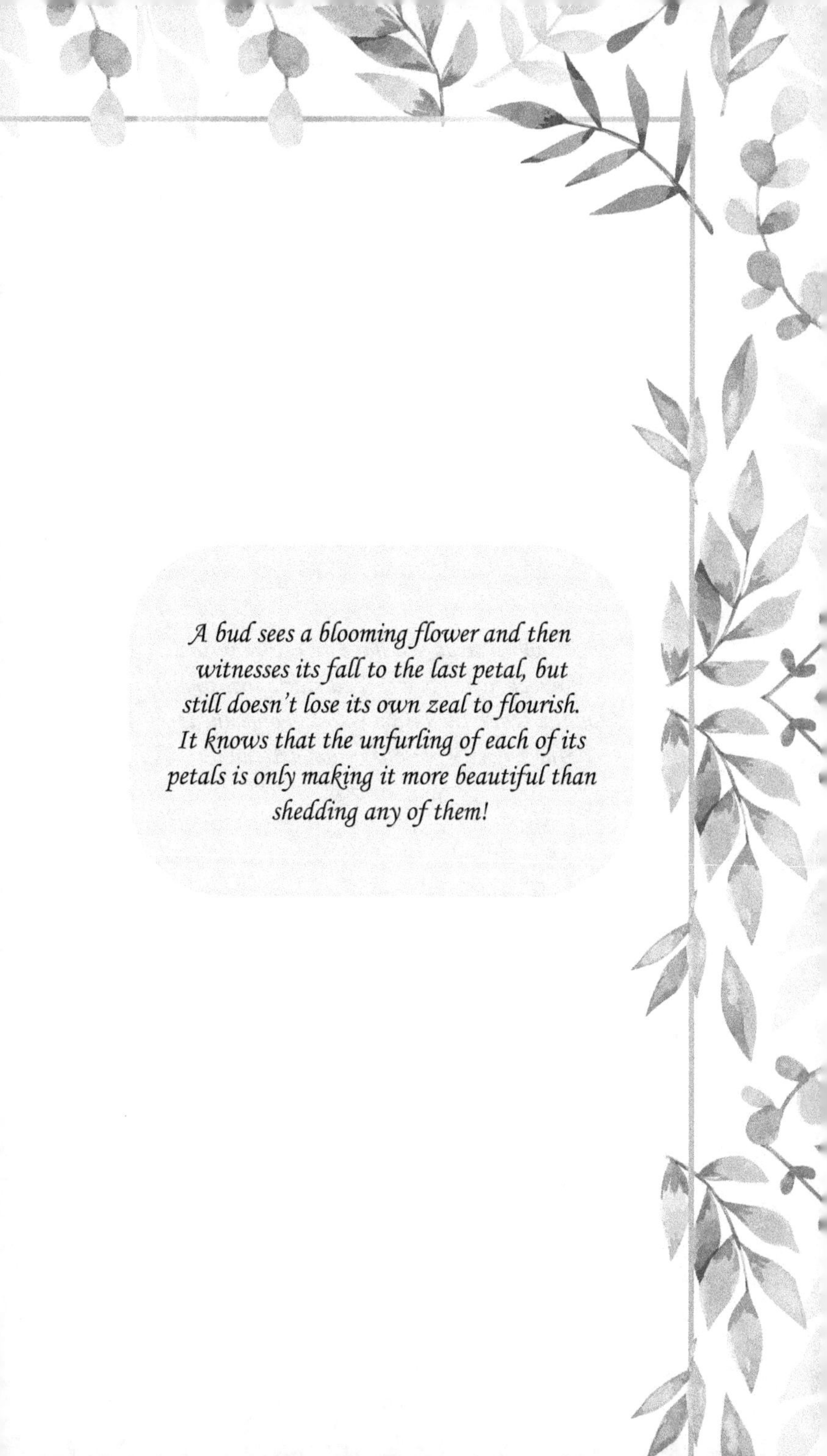

A bud sees a blooming flower and then witnesses its fall to the last petal, but still doesn't lose its own zeal to flourish. It knows that the unfurling of each of its petals is only making it more beautiful than shedding any of them!

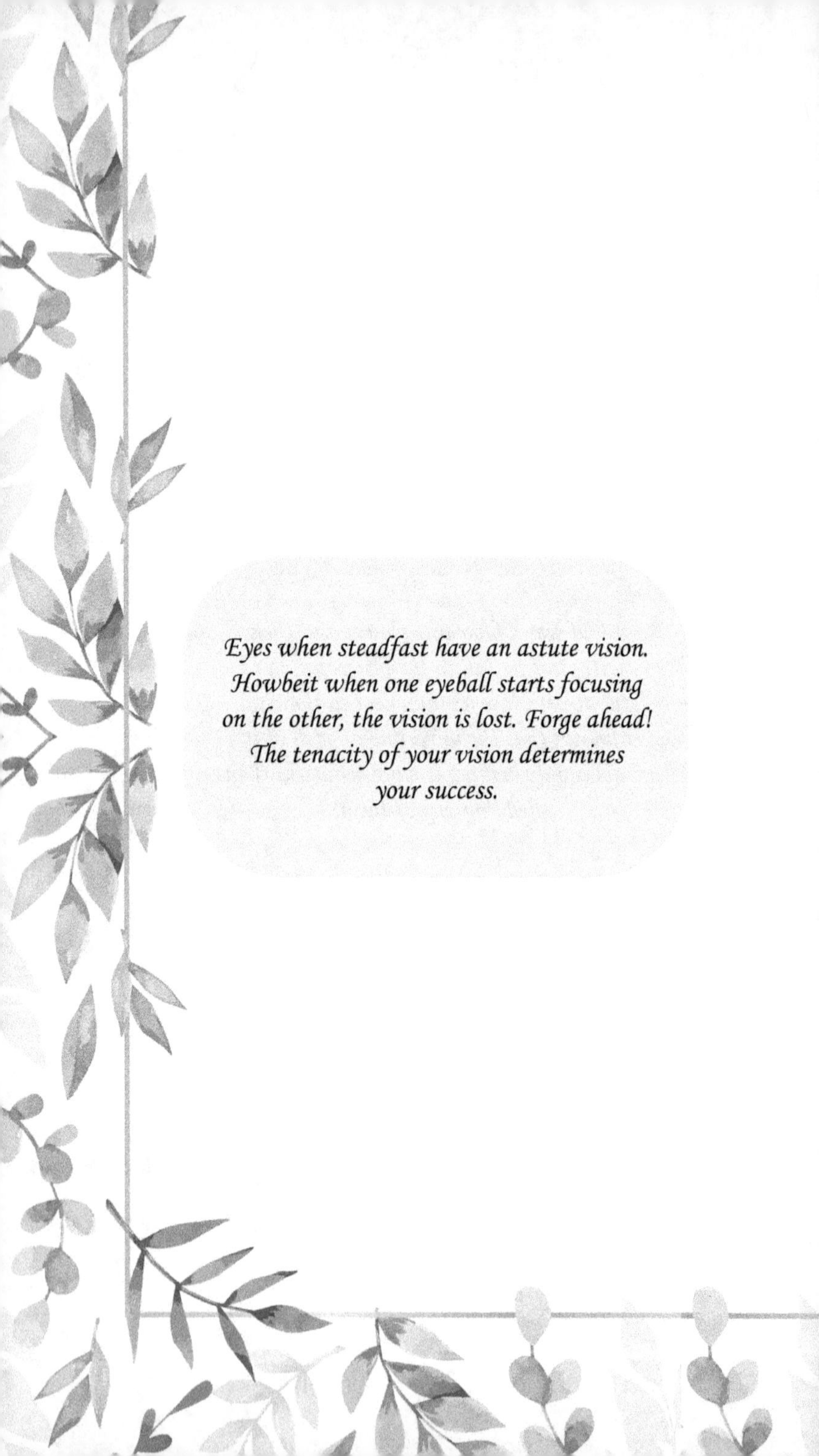

Eyes when steadfast have an astute vision. Howbeit when one eyeball starts focusing on the other, the vision is lost. Forge ahead! The tenacity of your vision determines your success.

Who says magic is only in magic? Try being a magician to your own life designedly and see how magic flows…

Don't try to copy anyone; masterpieces are always original!

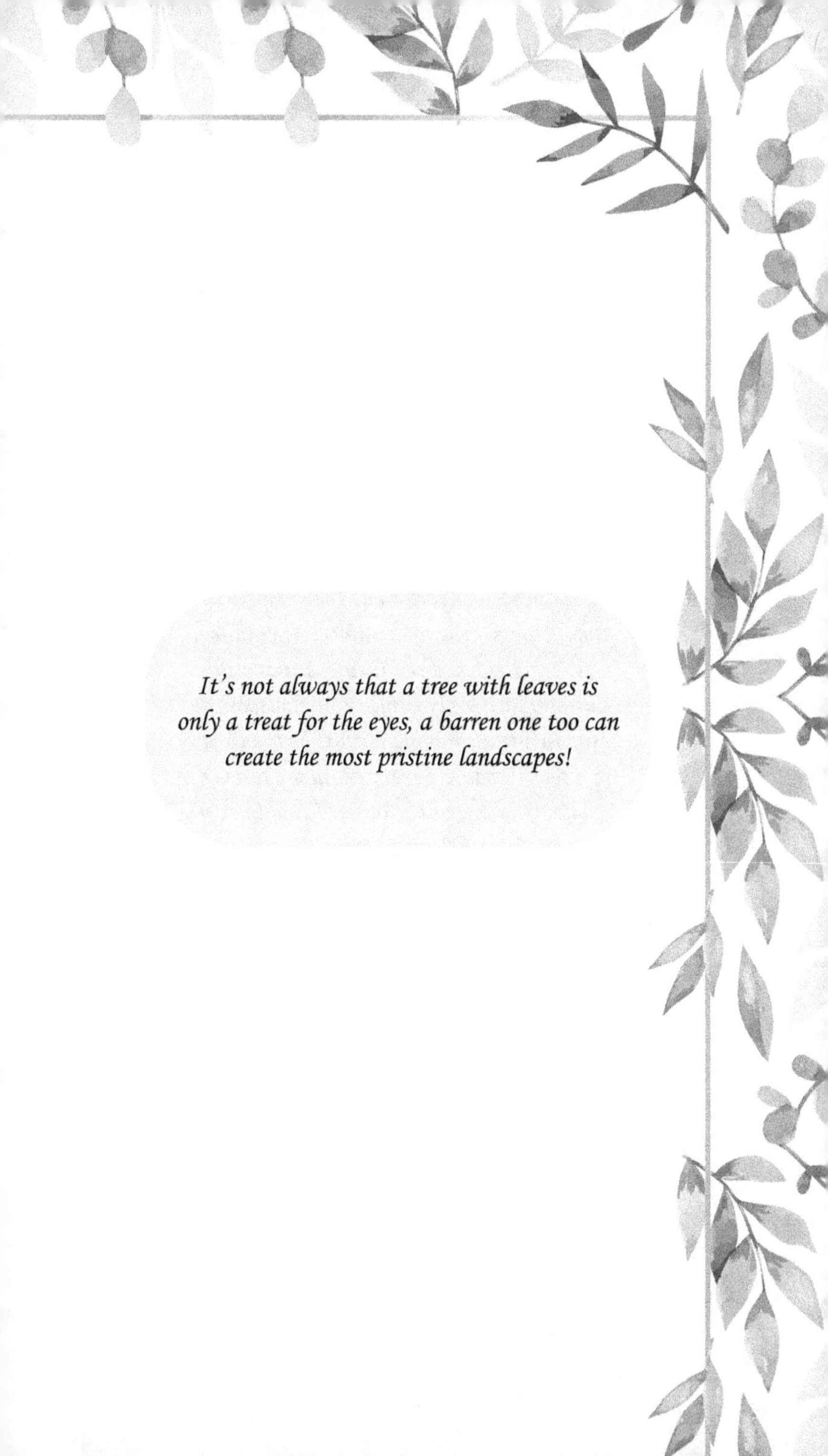

It's not always that a tree with leaves is only a treat for the eyes, a barren one too can create the most pristine landscapes!

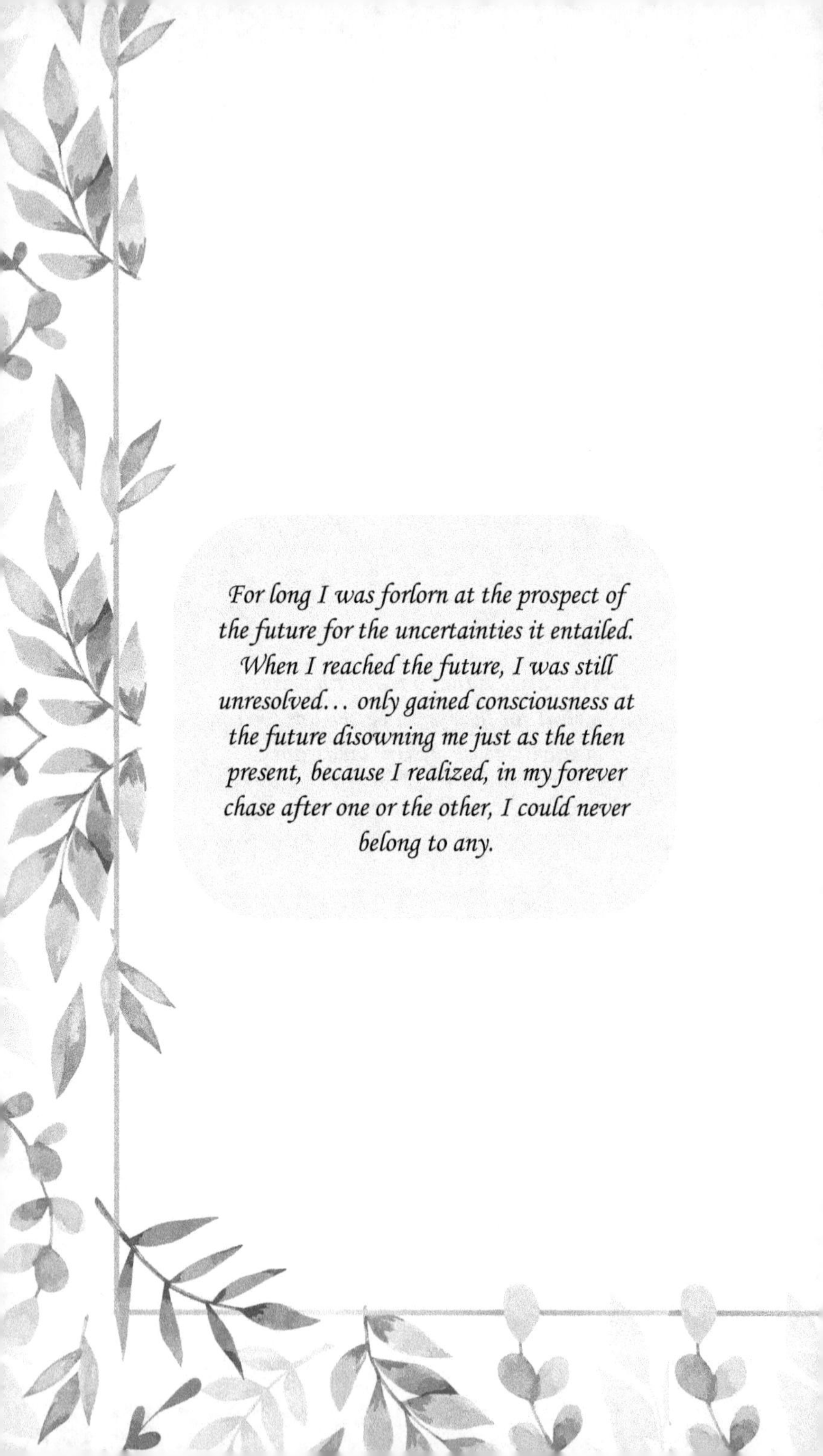

For long I was forlorn at the prospect of the future for the uncertainties it entailed. When I reached the future, I was still unresolved… only gained consciousness at the future disowning me just as the then present, because I realized, in my forever chase after one or the other, I could never belong to any.

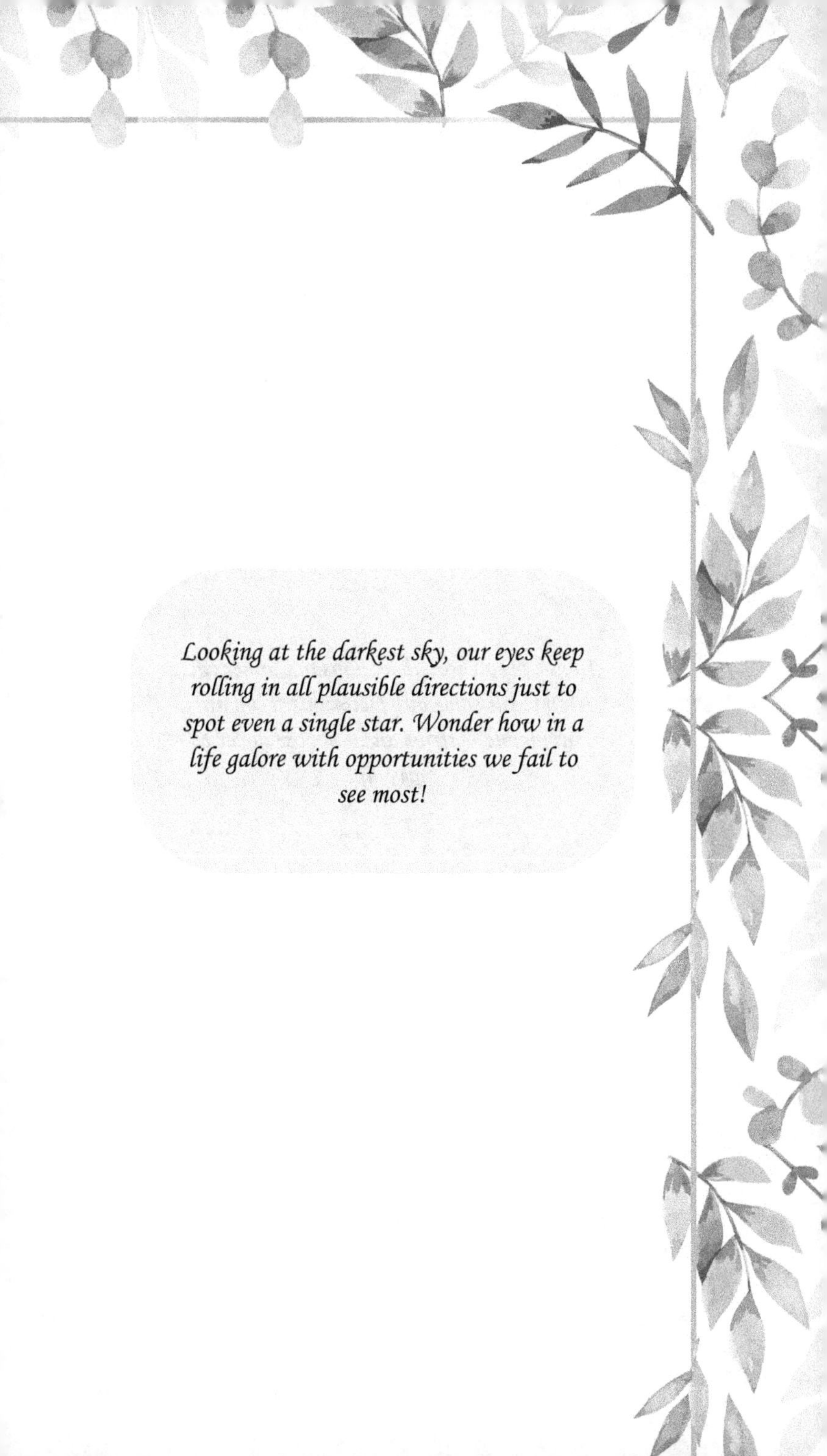

Looking at the darkest sky, our eyes keep rolling in all plausible directions just to spot even a single star. Wonder how in a life galore with opportunities we fail to see most!

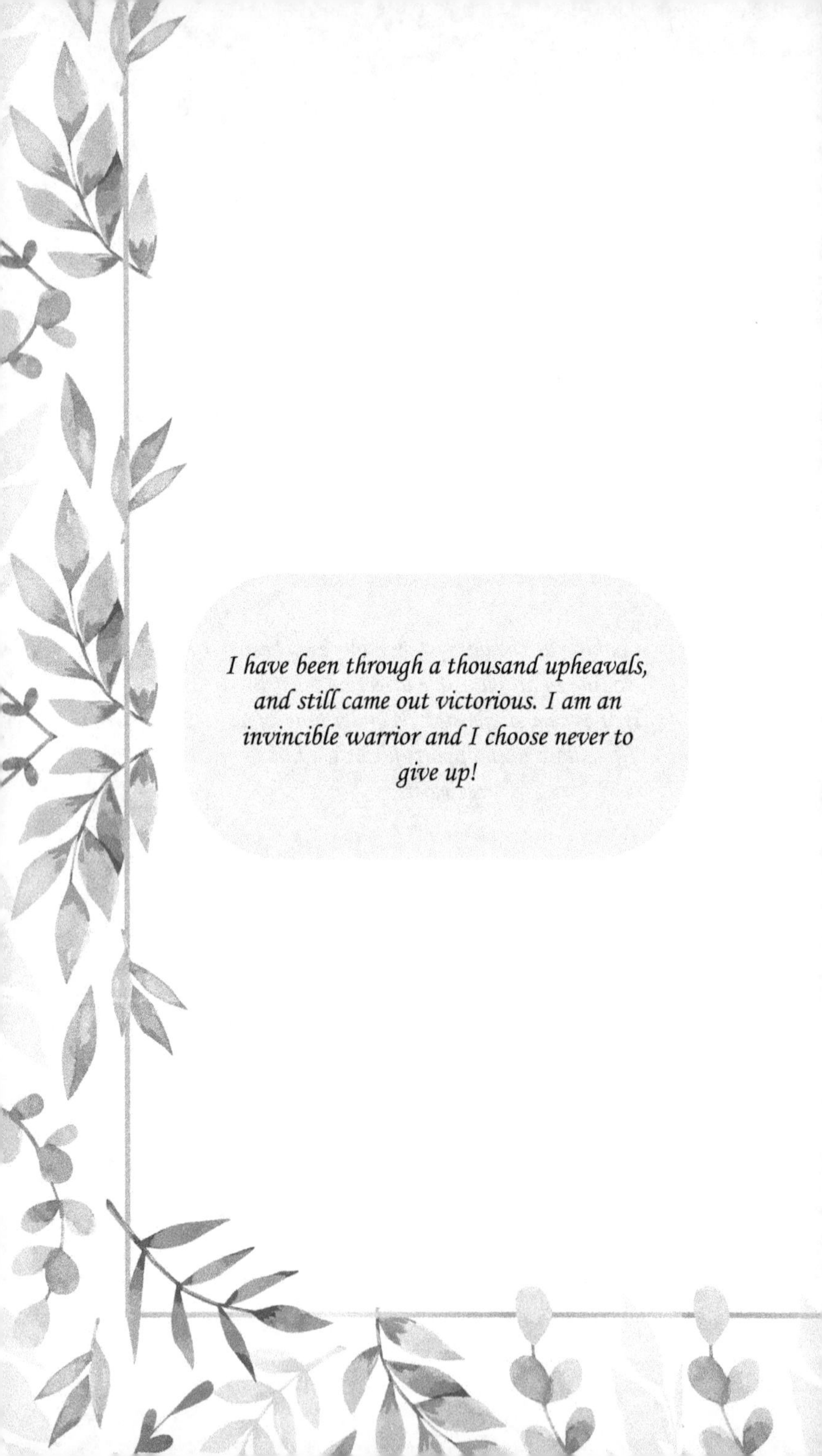

I have been through a thousand upheavals, and still came out victorious. I am an invincible warrior and I choose never to give up!

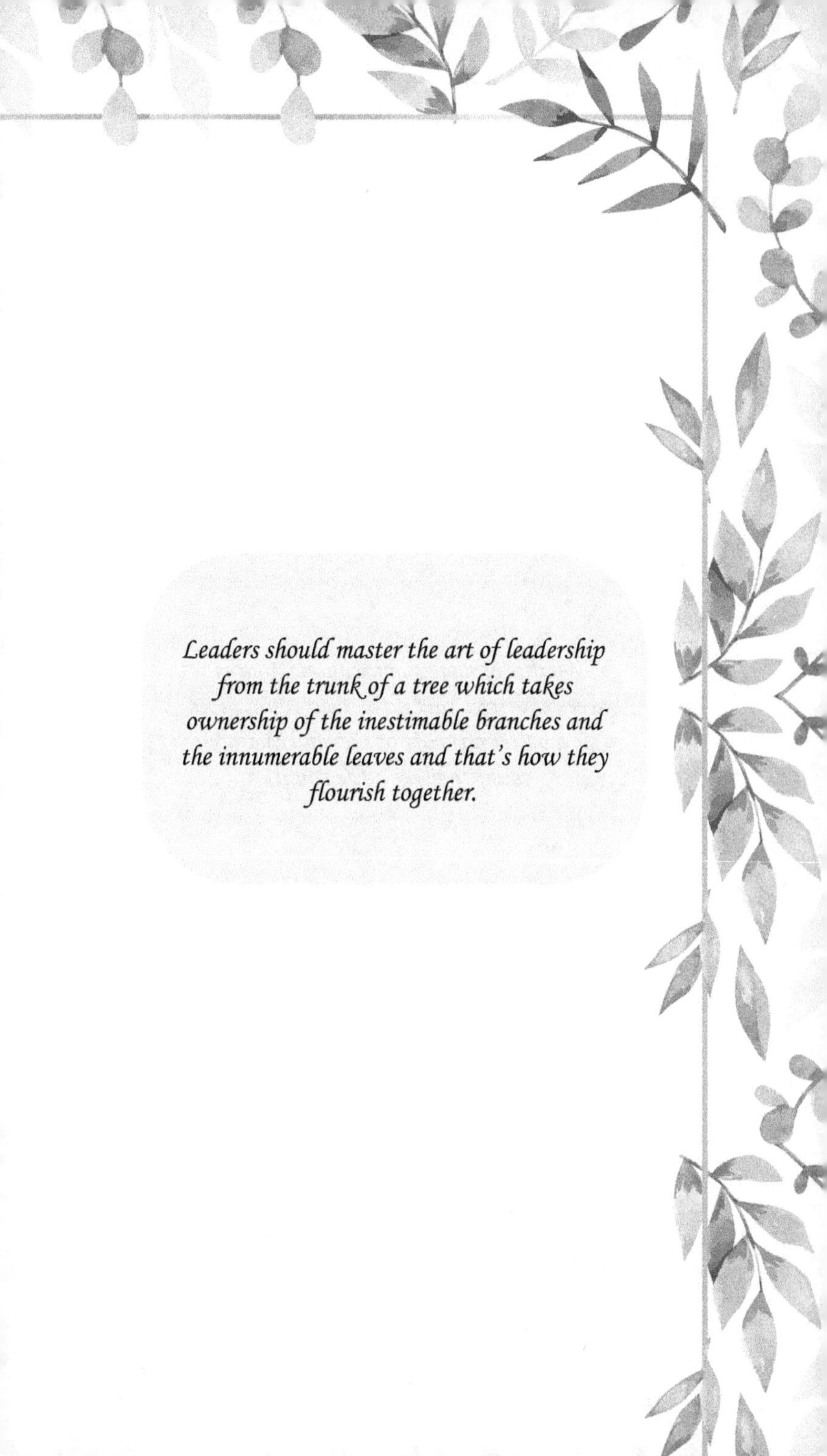

Leaders should master the art of leadership from the trunk of a tree which takes ownership of the inestimable branches and the innumerable leaves and that's how they flourish together.

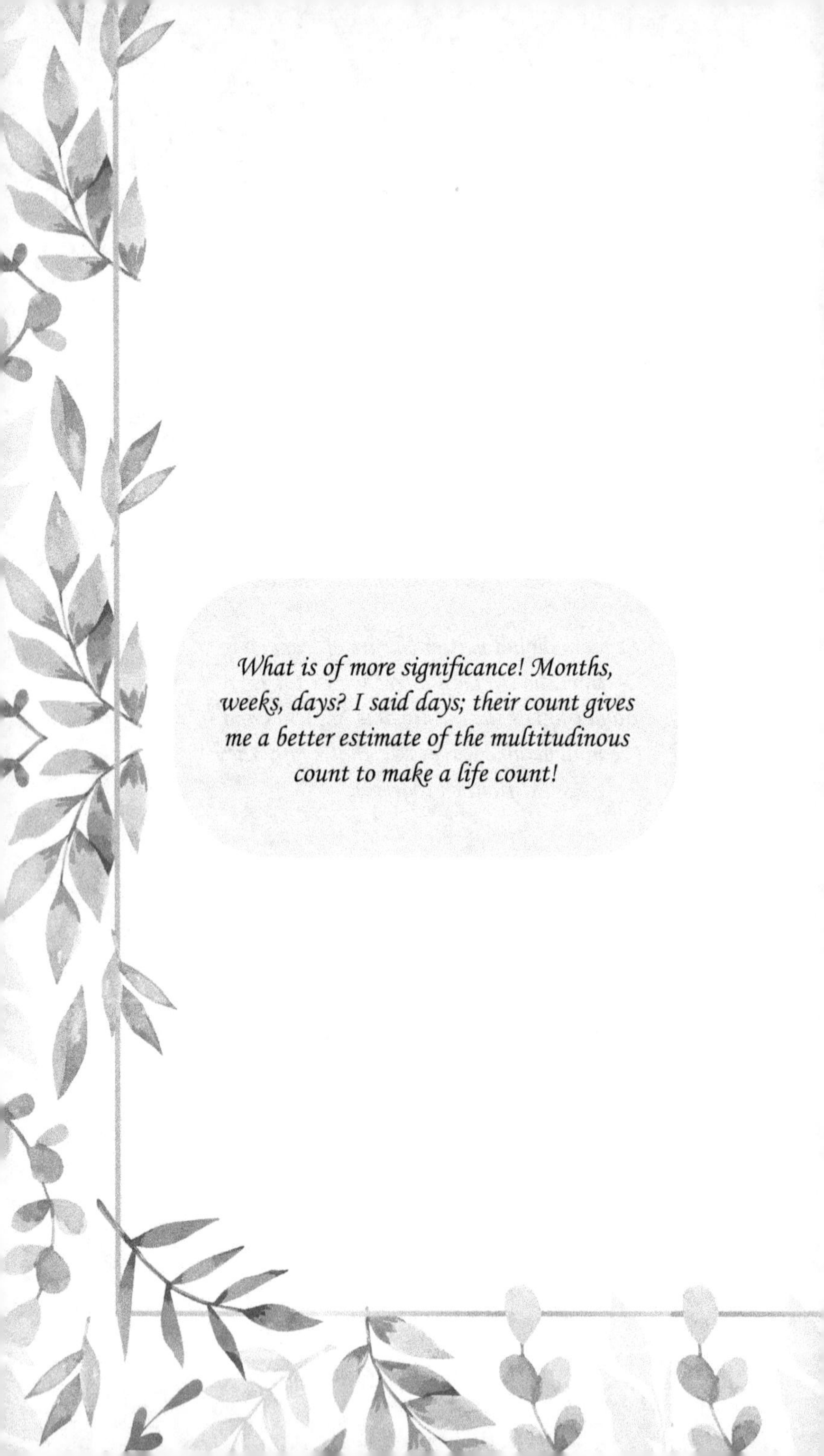

What is of more significance! Months, weeks, days? I said days; their count gives me a better estimate of the multitudinous count to make a life count!

*Basically you just need to keep going…
Everything else will fall in place! Isn't
this simple?*

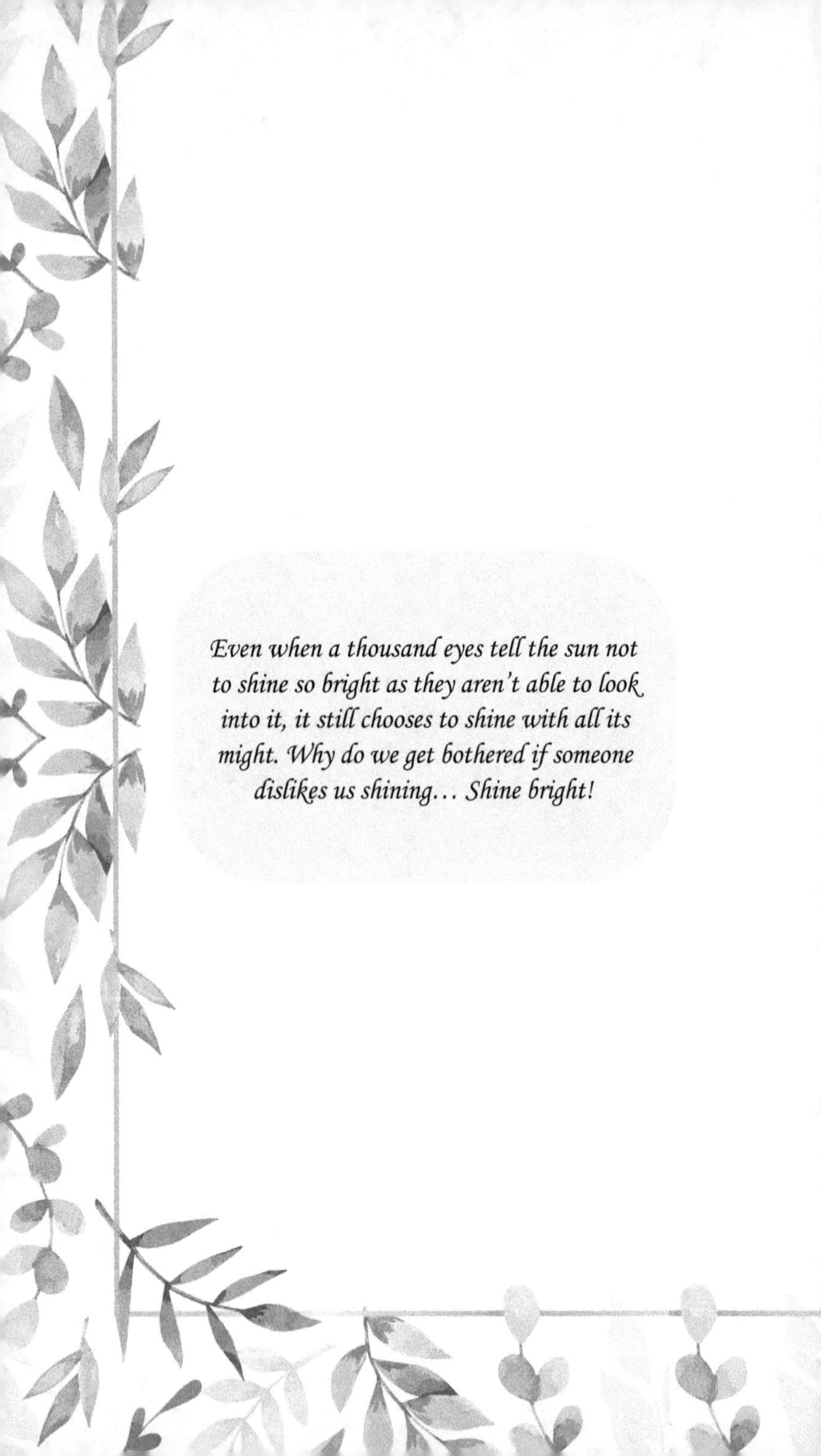

Even when a thousand eyes tell the sun not to shine so bright as they aren't able to look into it, it still chooses to shine with all its might. Why do we get bothered if someone dislikes us shining... Shine bright!

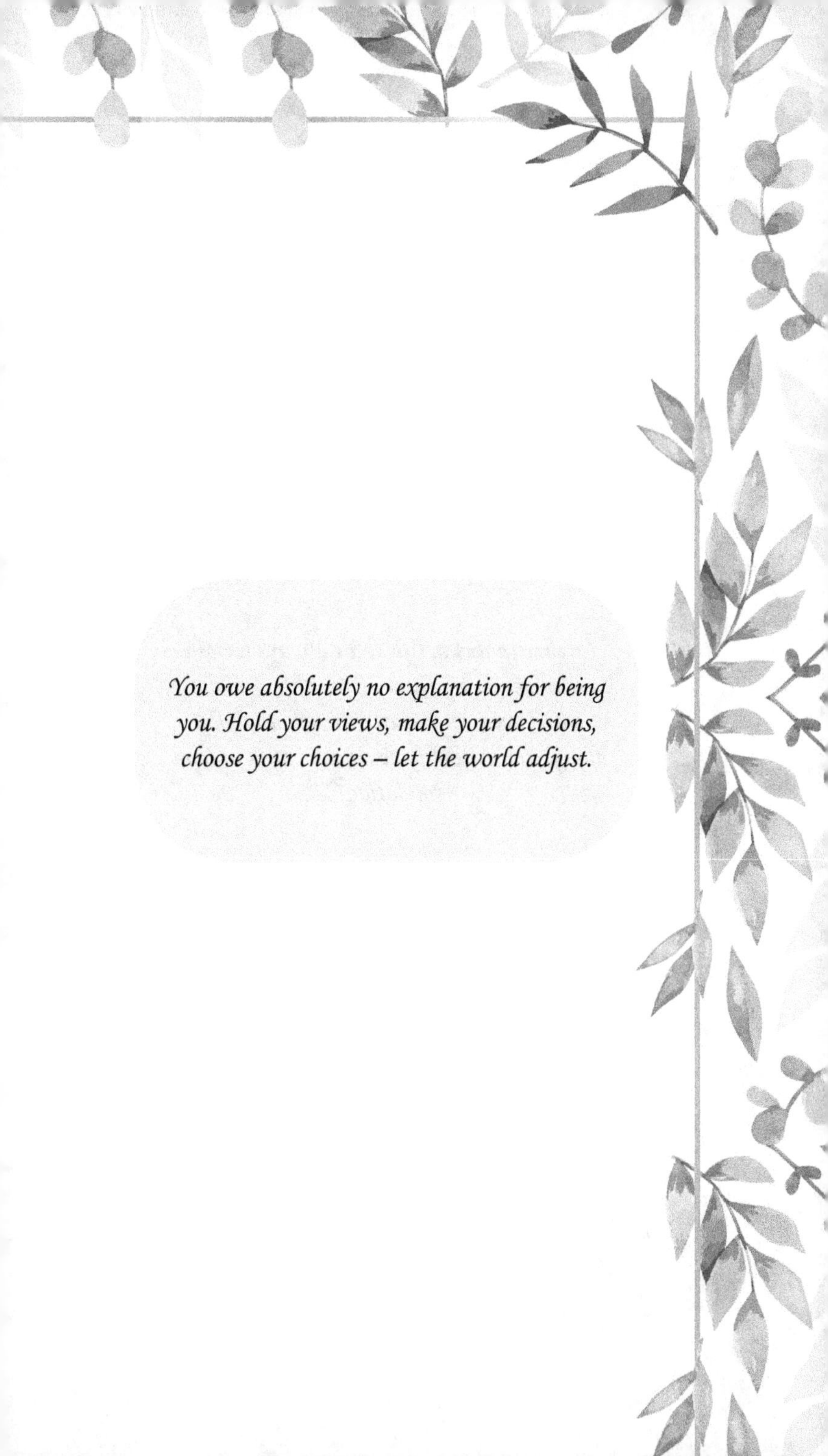

You owe absolutely no explanation for being you. Hold your views, make your decisions, choose your choices – let the world adjust.

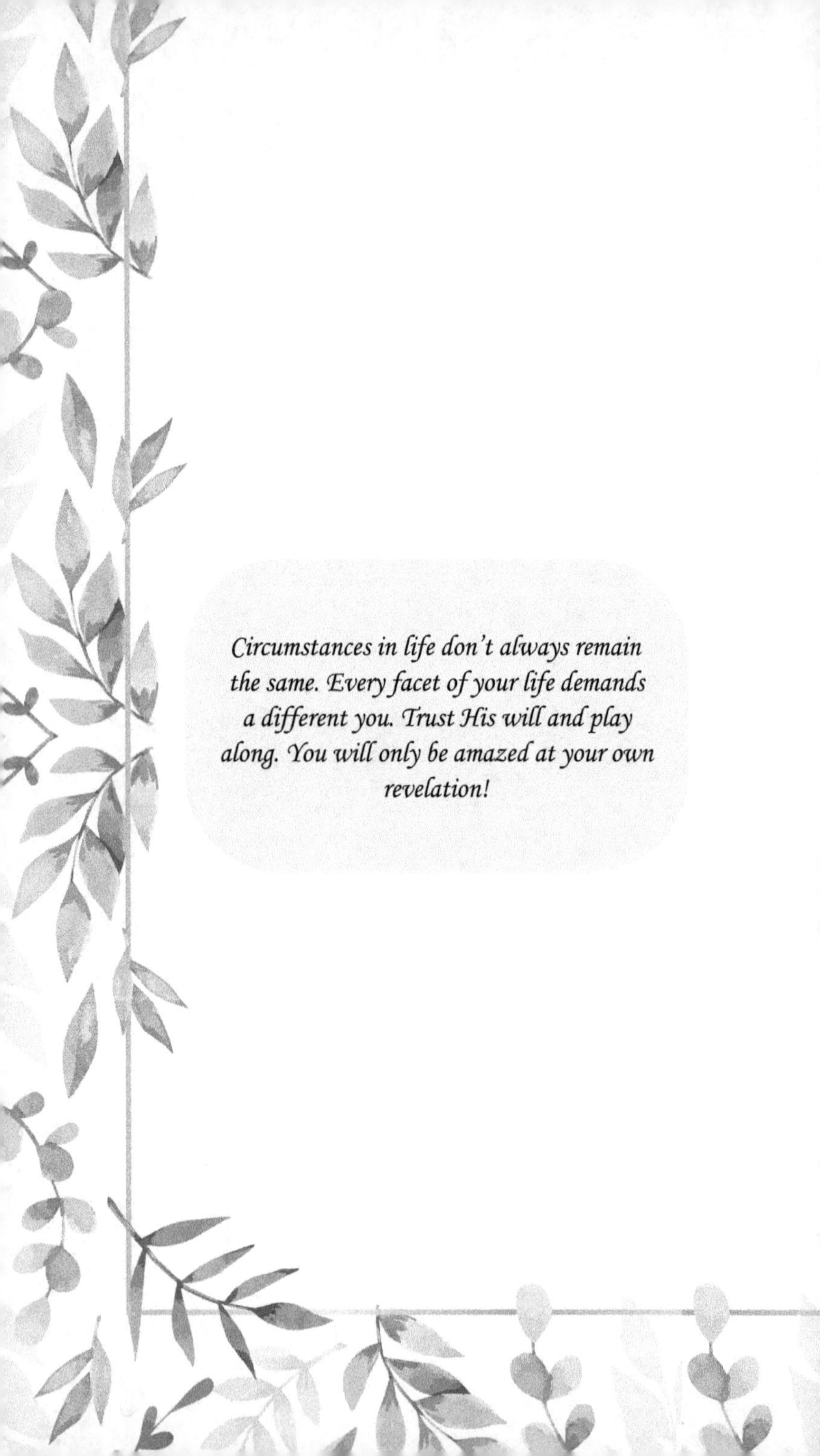

Circumstances in life don't always remain the same. Every facet of your life demands a different you. Trust His will and play along. You will only be amazed at your own revelation!

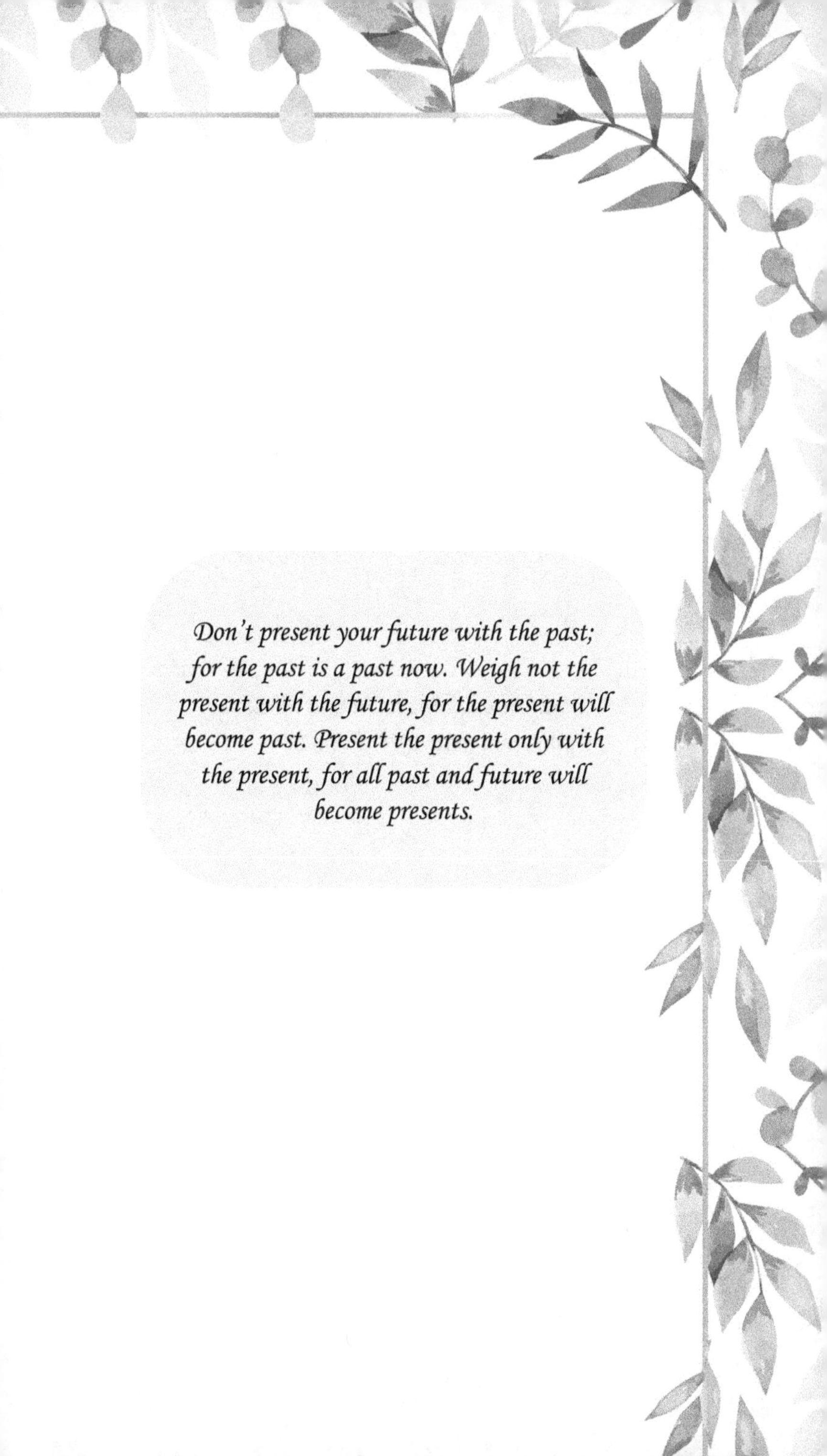

Don't present your future with the past; for the past is a past now. Weigh not the present with the future, for the present will become past. Present the present only with the present, for all past and future will become presents.

I heal through the night and that's my power! A new ray builds a new me!

Don't restrict the growth of a human mind by expectation of concordant views; the deliberations will lose the essence.

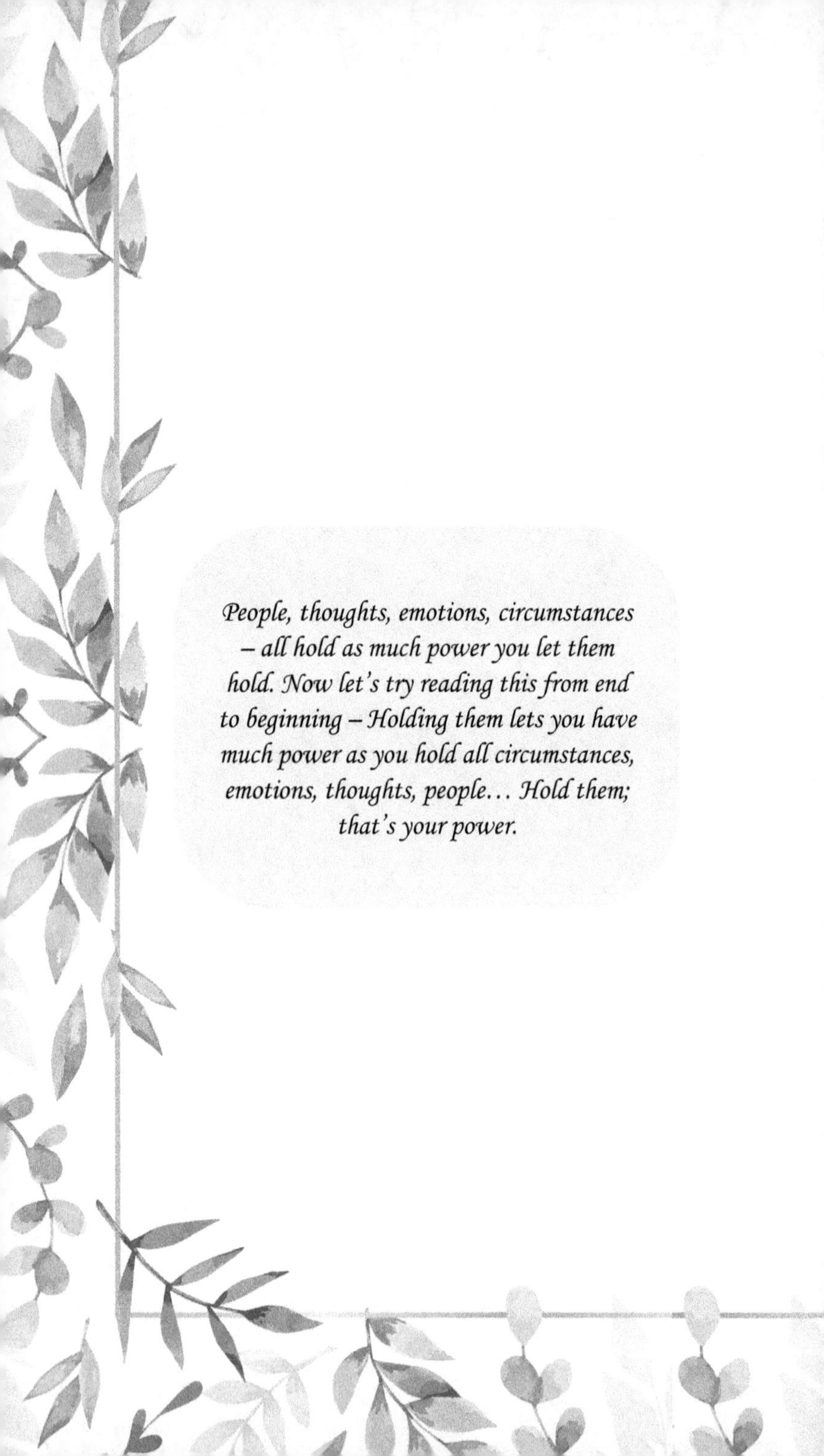

People, thoughts, emotions, circumstances – all hold as much power you let them hold. Now let's try reading this from end to beginning – Holding them lets you have much power as you hold all circumstances, emotions, thoughts, people… Hold them; that's your power.

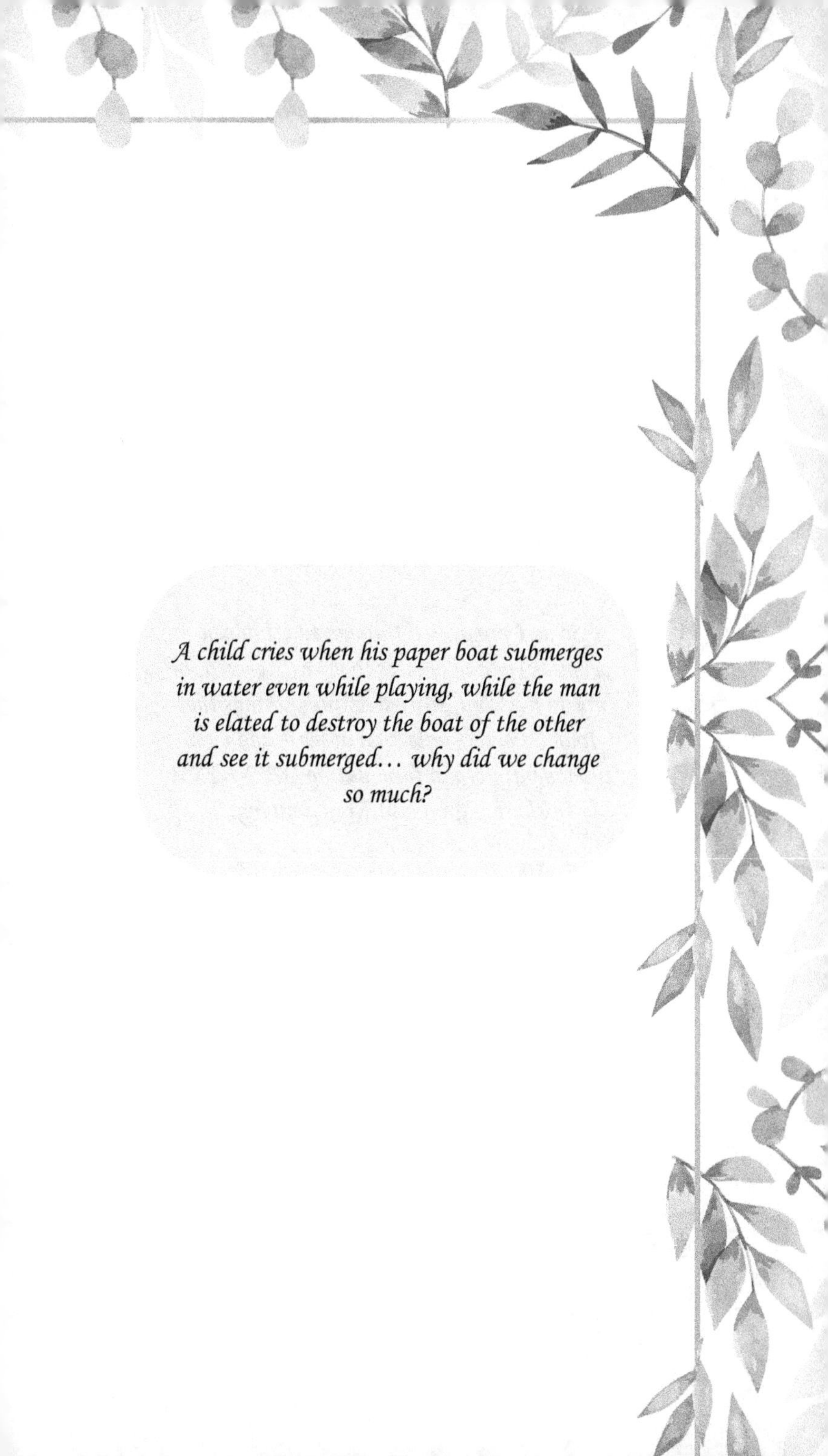

A child cries when his paper boat submerges in water even while playing, while the man is elated to destroy the boat of the other and see it submerged... why did we change so much?

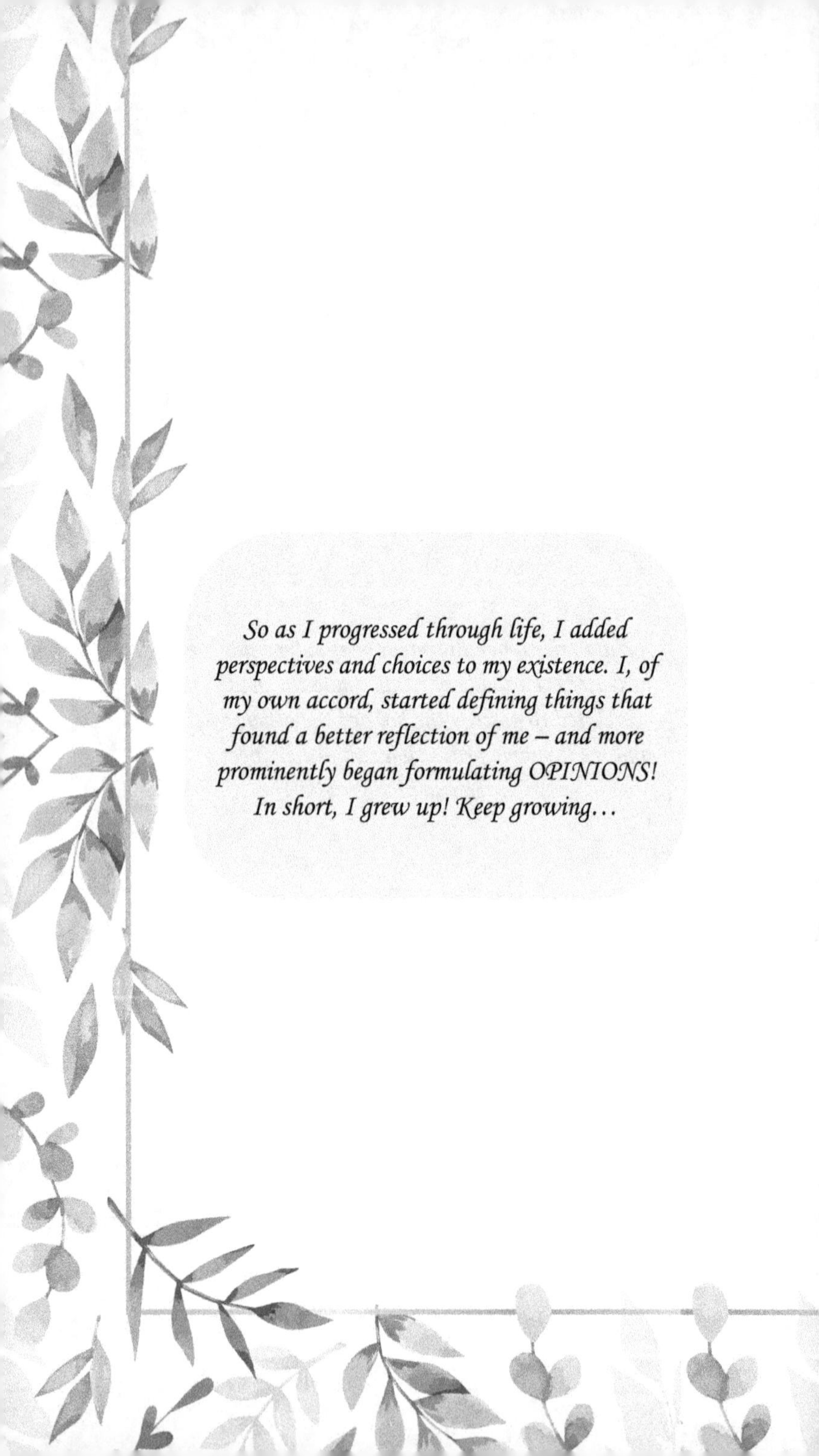

So as I progressed through life, I added perspectives and choices to my existence. I, of my own accord, started defining things that found a better reflection of me – and more prominently began formulating OPINIONS! In short, I grew up! Keep growing…

Some say the creaking of a candle is the cry the candle cries because it is burning. Well, I say that's the music it plays for you to revel in its light… illuminate!

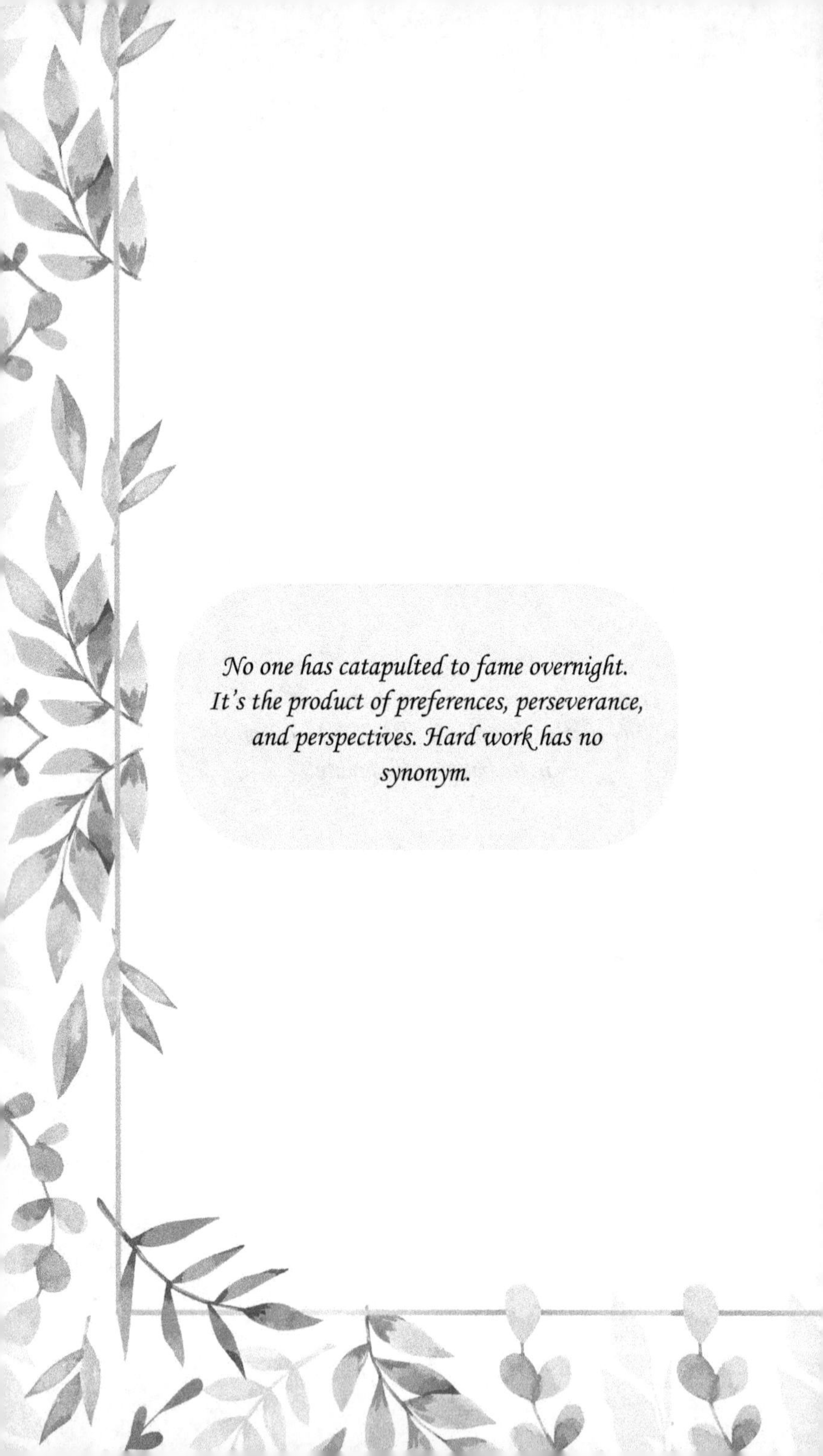

No one has catapulted to fame overnight. It's the product of preferences, perseverance, and perspectives. Hard work has no synonym.

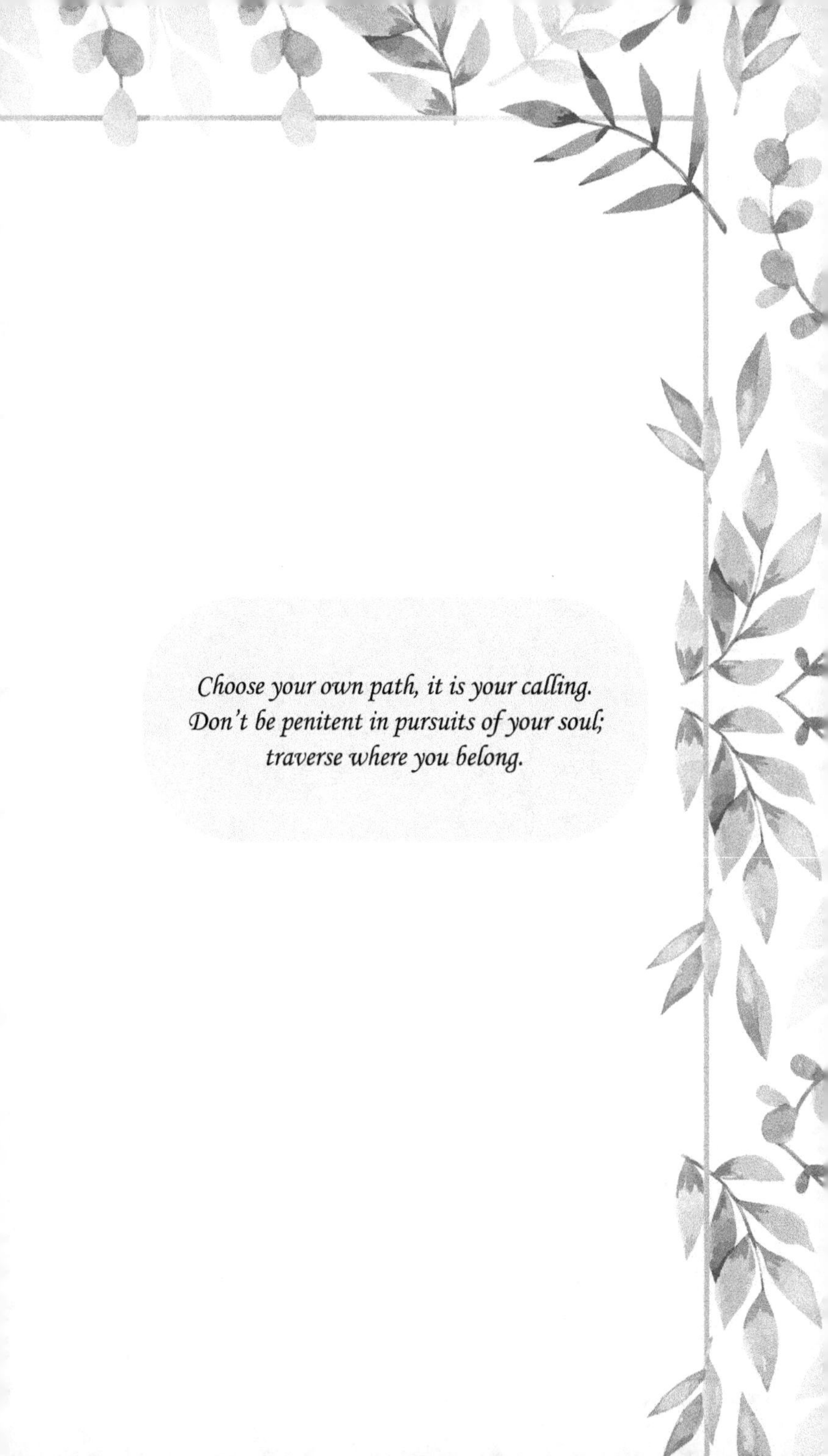

Choose your own path, it is your calling.
Don't be penitent in pursuits of your soul;
traverse where you belong.

An attempt to time the time is futile; venture to make the most of time and amaze how time makes time.

The sun that falls on nature brightens it,
the light that falls on darkness lightens it,
then why do I hold back my own light to
glisten?

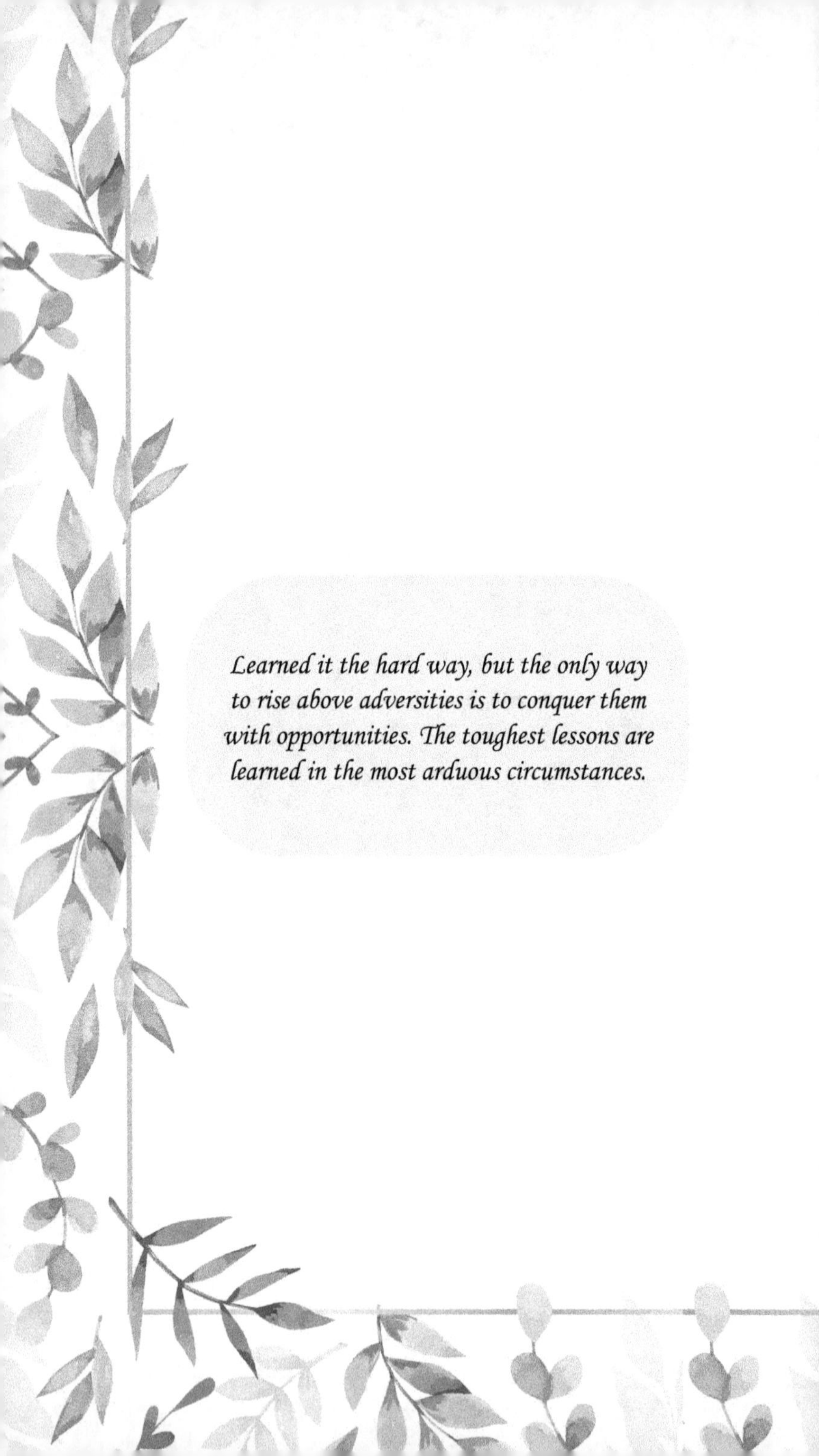

Learned it the hard way, but the only way to rise above adversities is to conquer them with opportunities. The toughest lessons are learned in the most arduous circumstances.

The potential to change a negative situation to a positive one determines your strength.

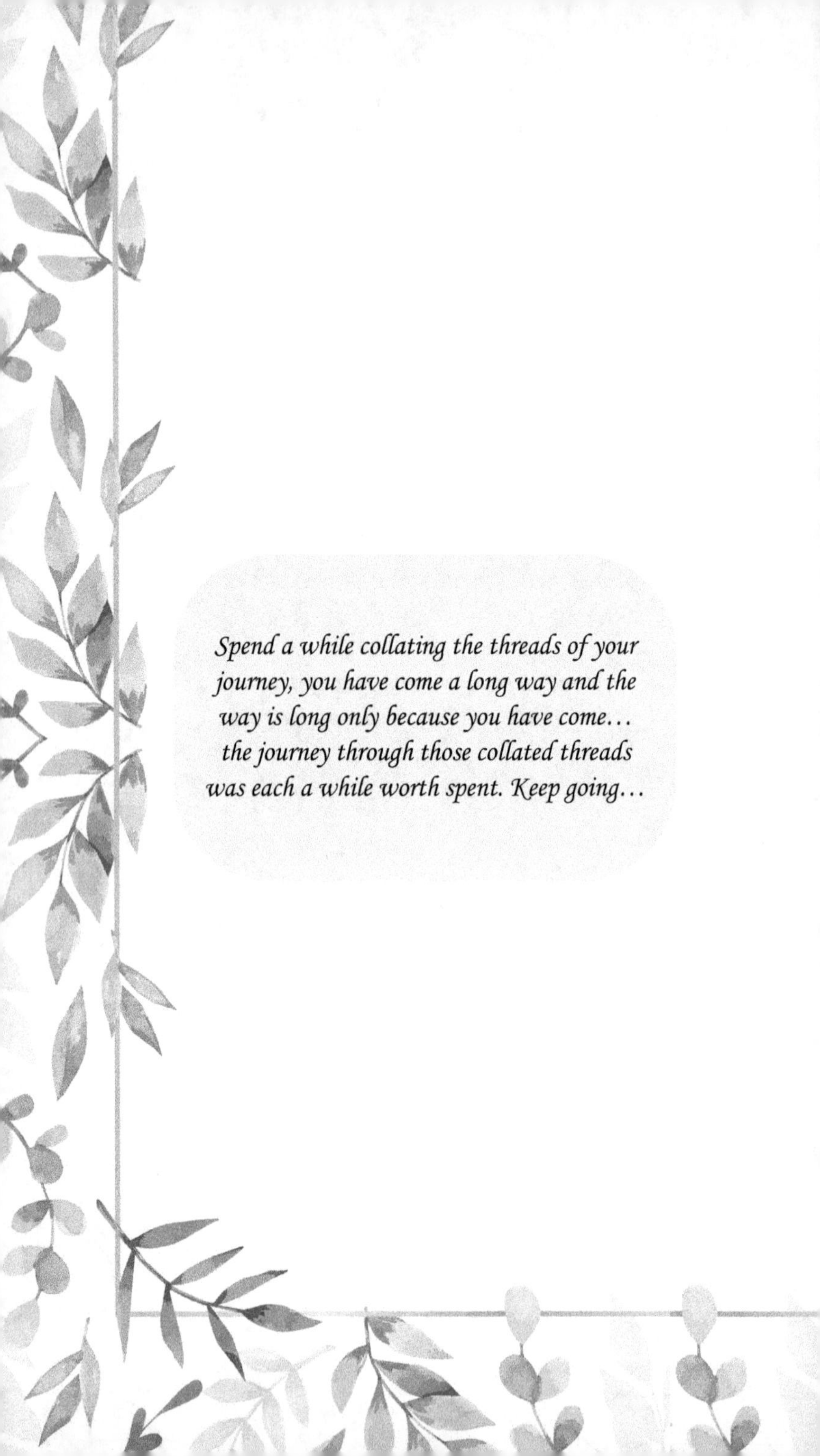

Spend a while collating the threads of your journey, you have come a long way and the way is long only because you have come… the journey through those collated threads was each a while worth spent. Keep going…

One opportunity paves way for the other; you only need to open your eyes and look around.

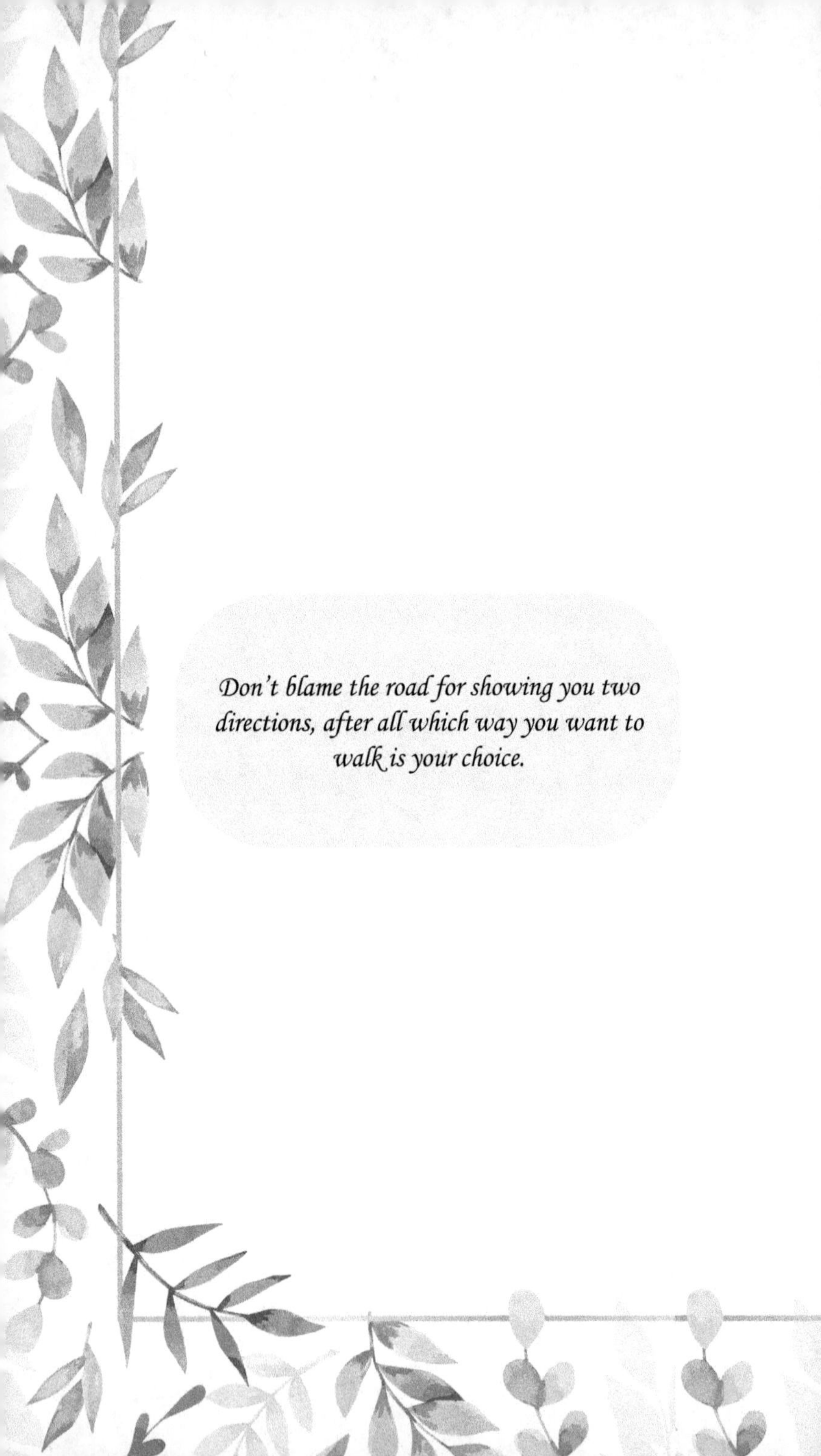
Don't blame the road for showing you two directions, after all which way you want to walk is your choice.

Strength and weakness to me have always been synonymous; for I let my weaknesses unveil my strengths and never let my strengths yield to my weaknesses.

Meditate. There's nothing more beautiful than being with yourself.

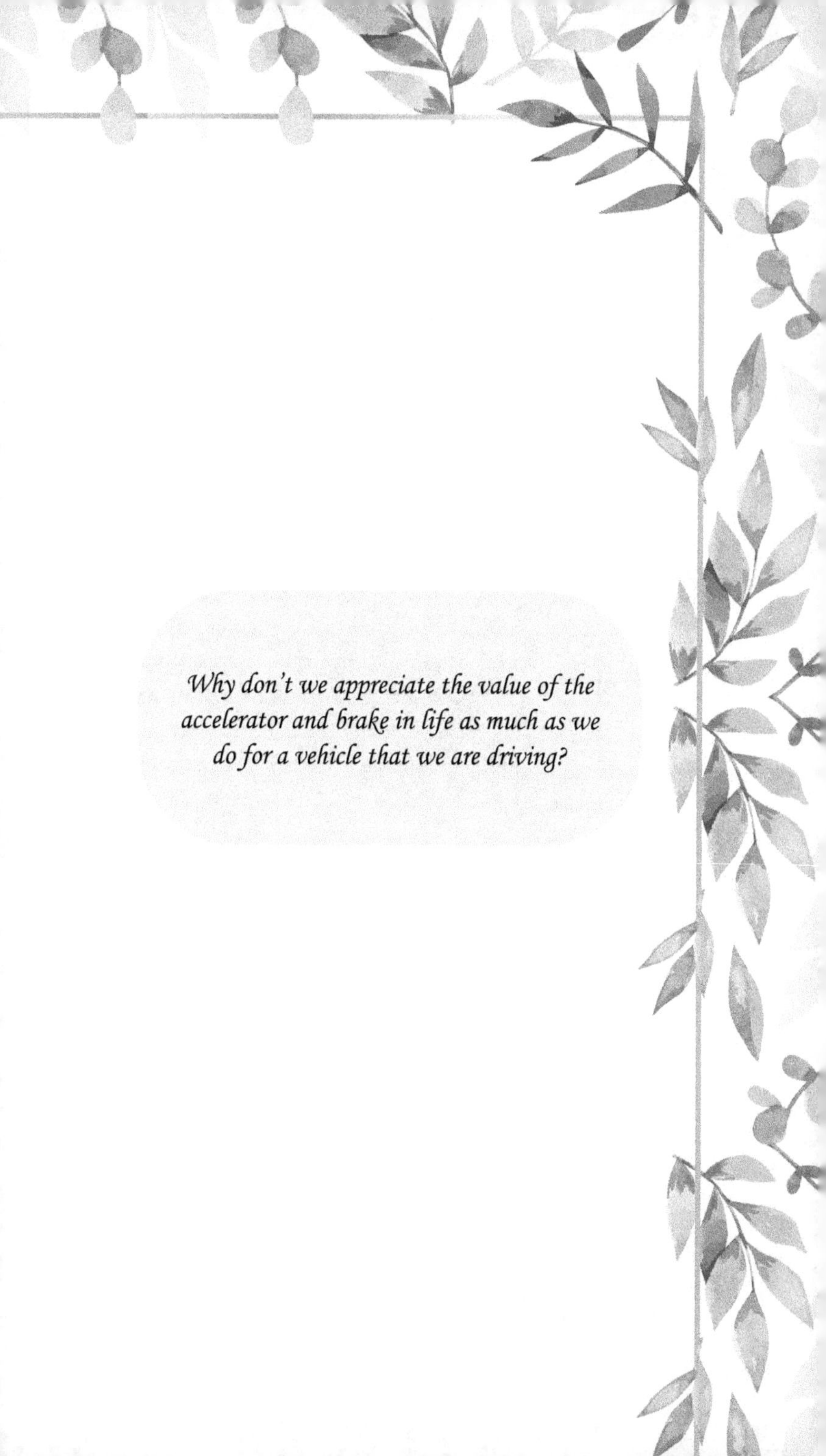

Why don't we appreciate the value of the accelerator and brake in life as much as we do for a vehicle that we are driving?

While a chance is a matter of choice, a choice is never a matter of chance. Take a chance, but make the right choice.

Travel. Wander. Explore. It rejuvenates your soul.

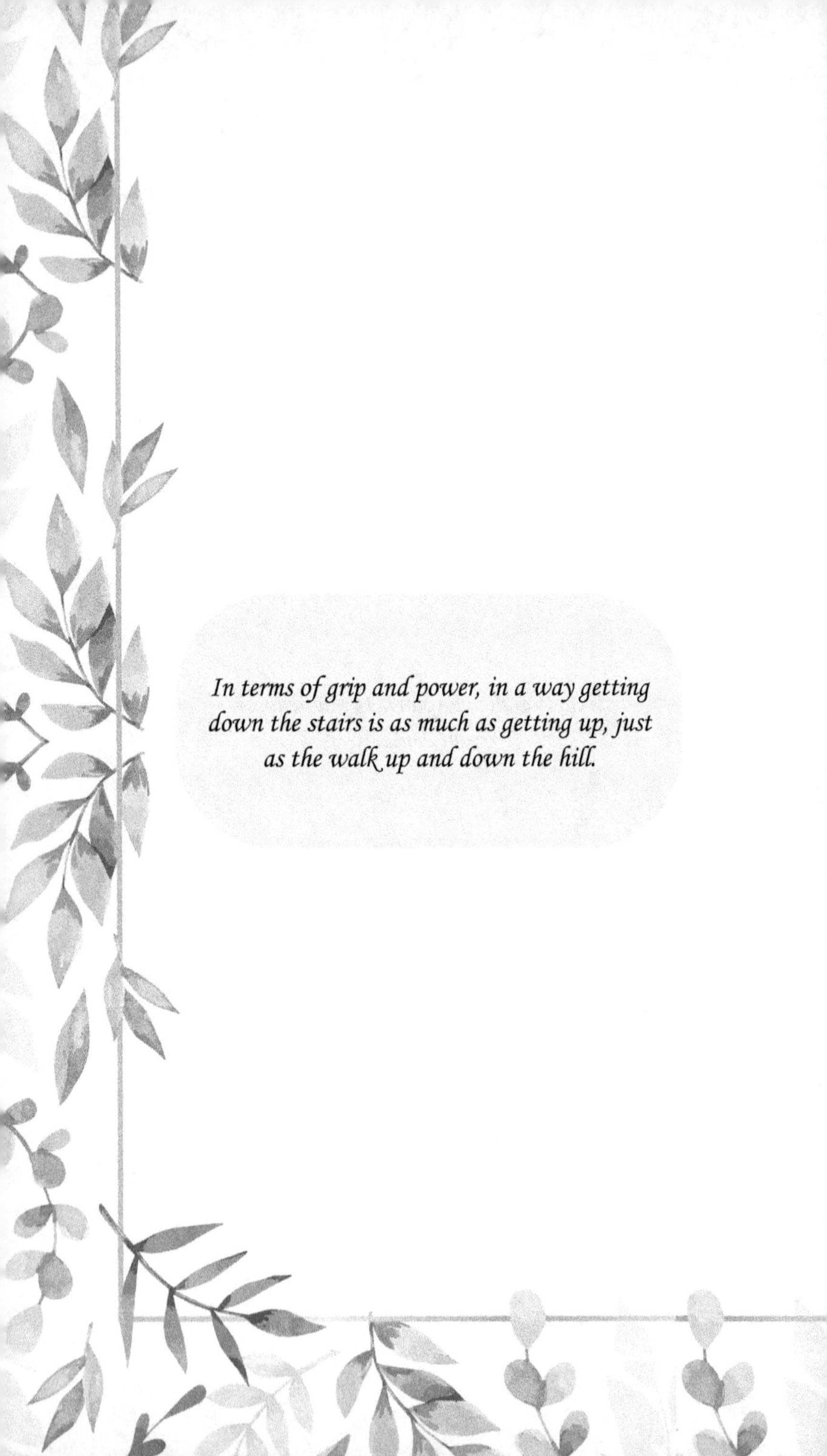

In terms of grip and power, in a way getting down the stairs is as much as getting up, just as the walk up and down the hill.

Roots let the tree bear leaves again, just as your strengths let your weaknesses bear strength again.

Love brings out the best in you; if it brings out the worst, it isn't love. Move on…

Take each day at a time. And if that's also getting too much to endure; try just with a moment.

The chirping birds, the gushing water, the breezy wind, the gigantic mountains are lessons enough for those who want to learn.

Sing a song, dance a dance, smile the most beautiful smile – in short; LIVE!

Through thinking a thought; don't let the thought think through you!

It took millions of seconds to build that courage in you, don't let a minute of fear overpower that.

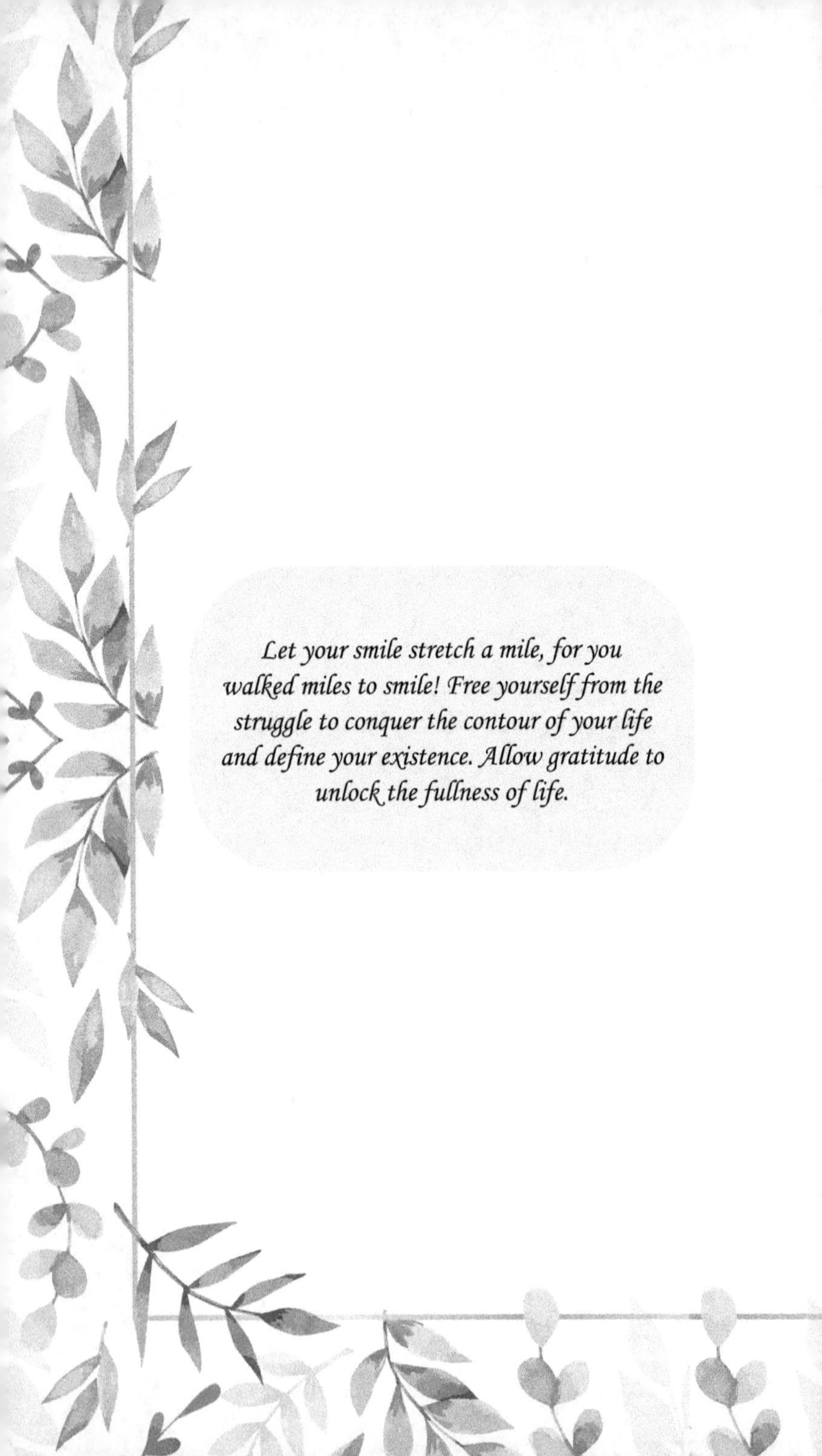

Let your smile stretch a mile, for you walked miles to smile! Free yourself from the struggle to conquer the contour of your life and define your existence. Allow gratitude to unlock the fullness of life.

I was pacing up and down the memory lane not sure if I was chasing the memories or the memories were chasing me.

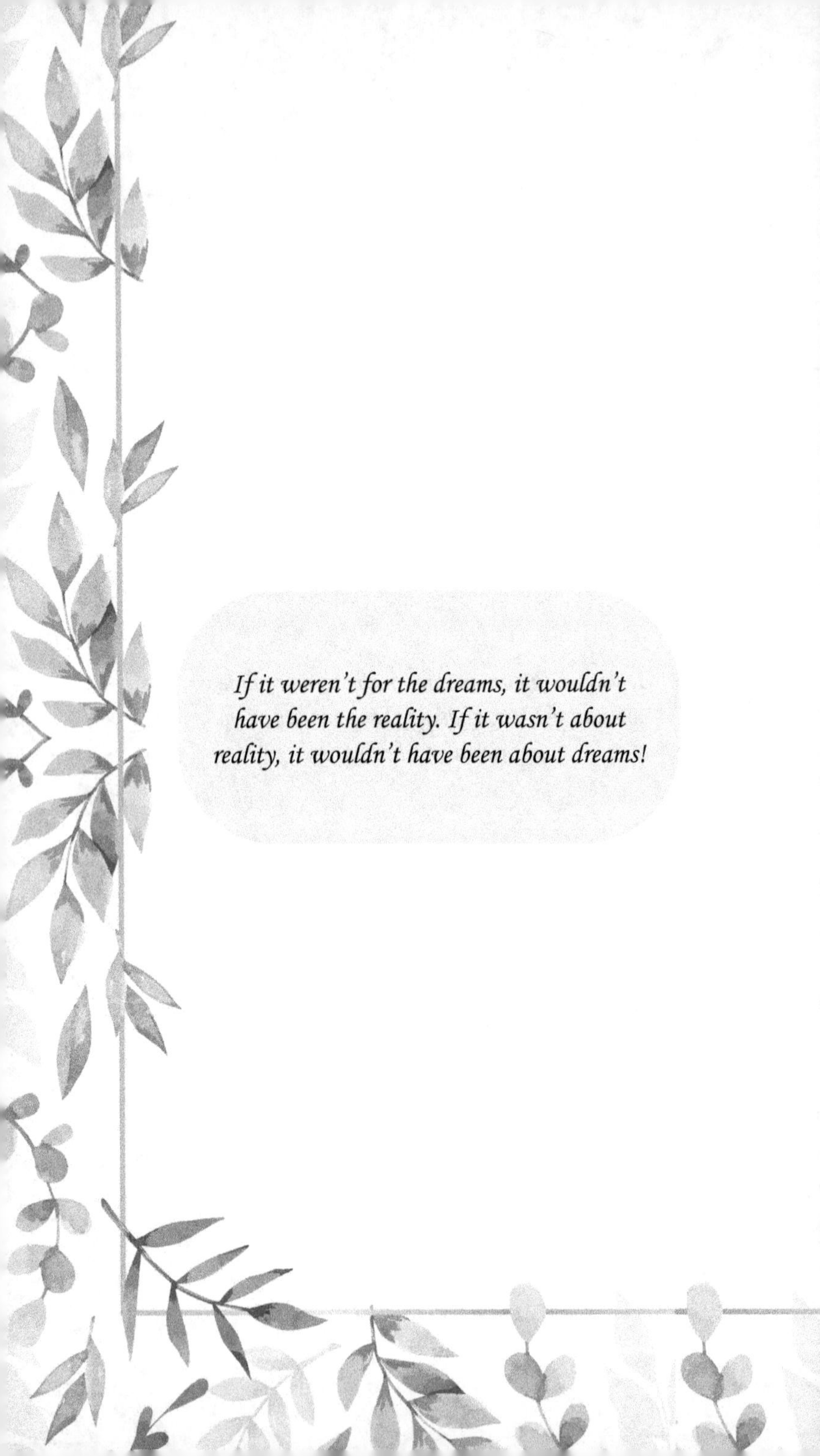

If it weren't for the dreams, it wouldn't have been the reality. If it wasn't about reality, it wouldn't have been about dreams!

It's not that wisdom is in solitude. The real victory is in conquering solitude with wisdom.

Calm your mind. Settle the restlessness…
Breathe!

Sight your priorities right before you lose sight of your priorities being right.

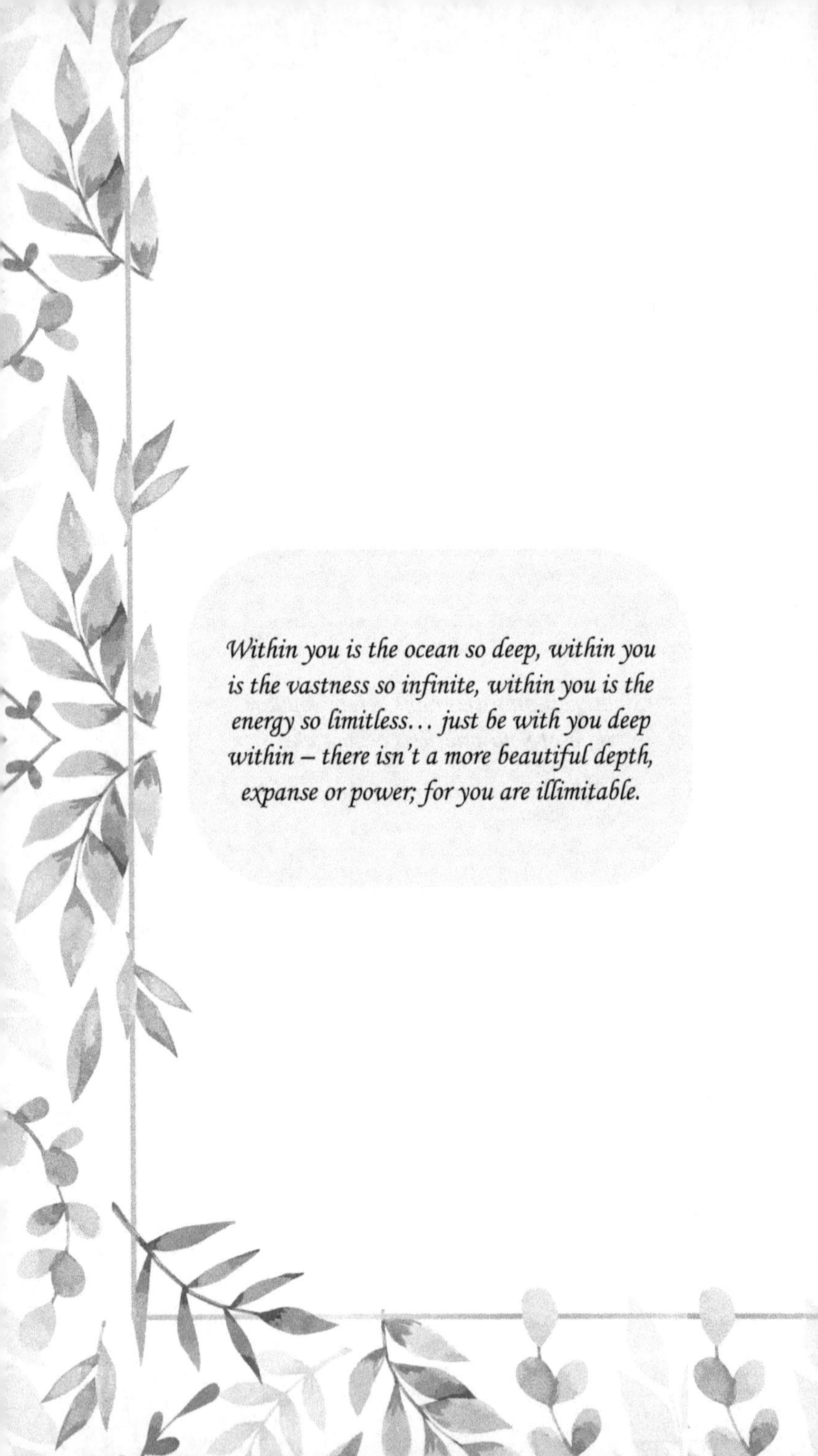

Within you is the ocean so deep, within you is the vastness so infinite, within you is the energy so limitless… just be with you deep within – there isn't a more beautiful depth, expanse or power; for you are illimitable.

Chance encounters can create the most soulful bonds only because we give them a chance rather than encountering them with a bond that our souls want to create.

Within me is the power with me without which I will be out of all power with me.

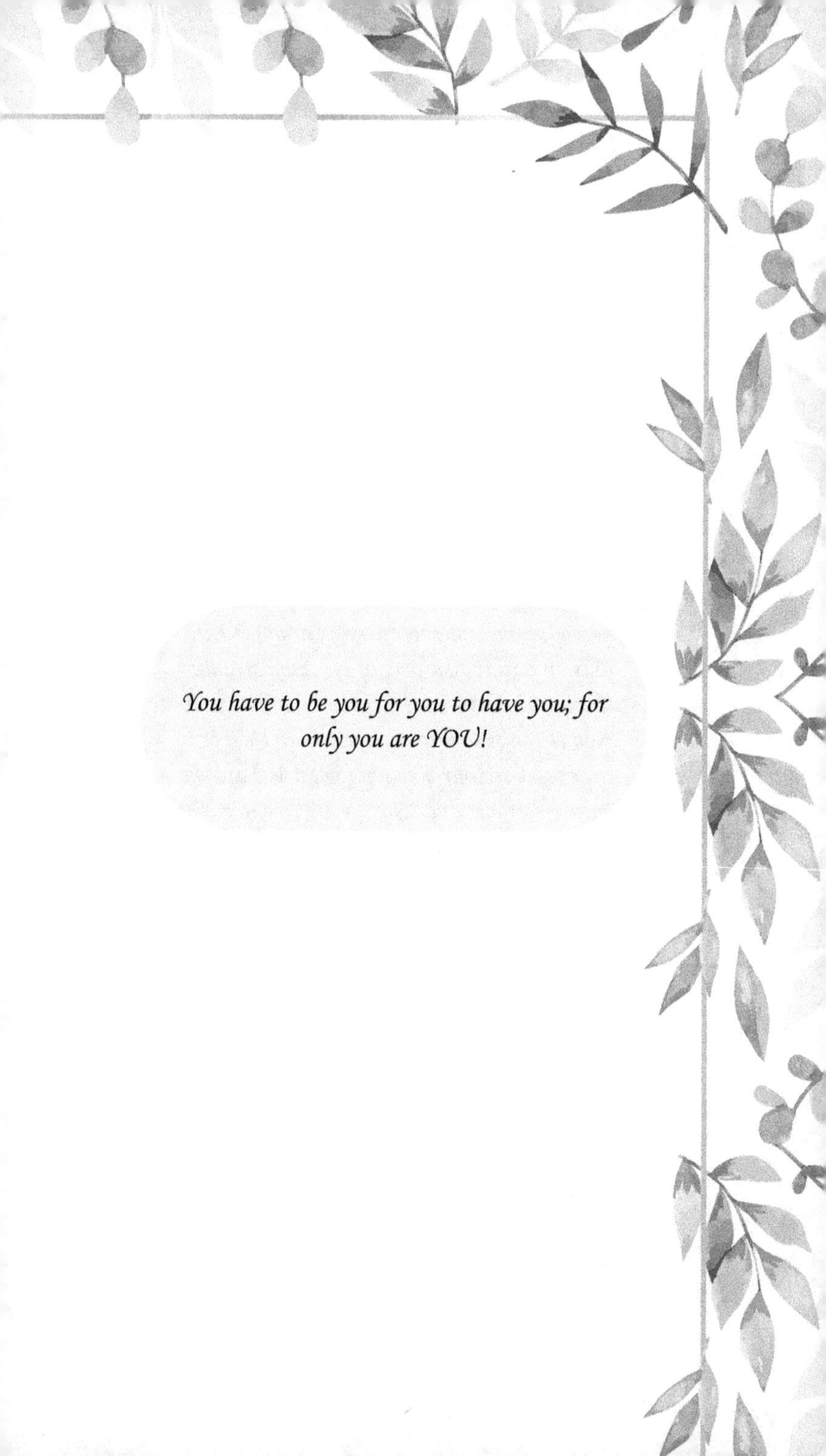

You have to be you for you to have you; for only you are YOU!

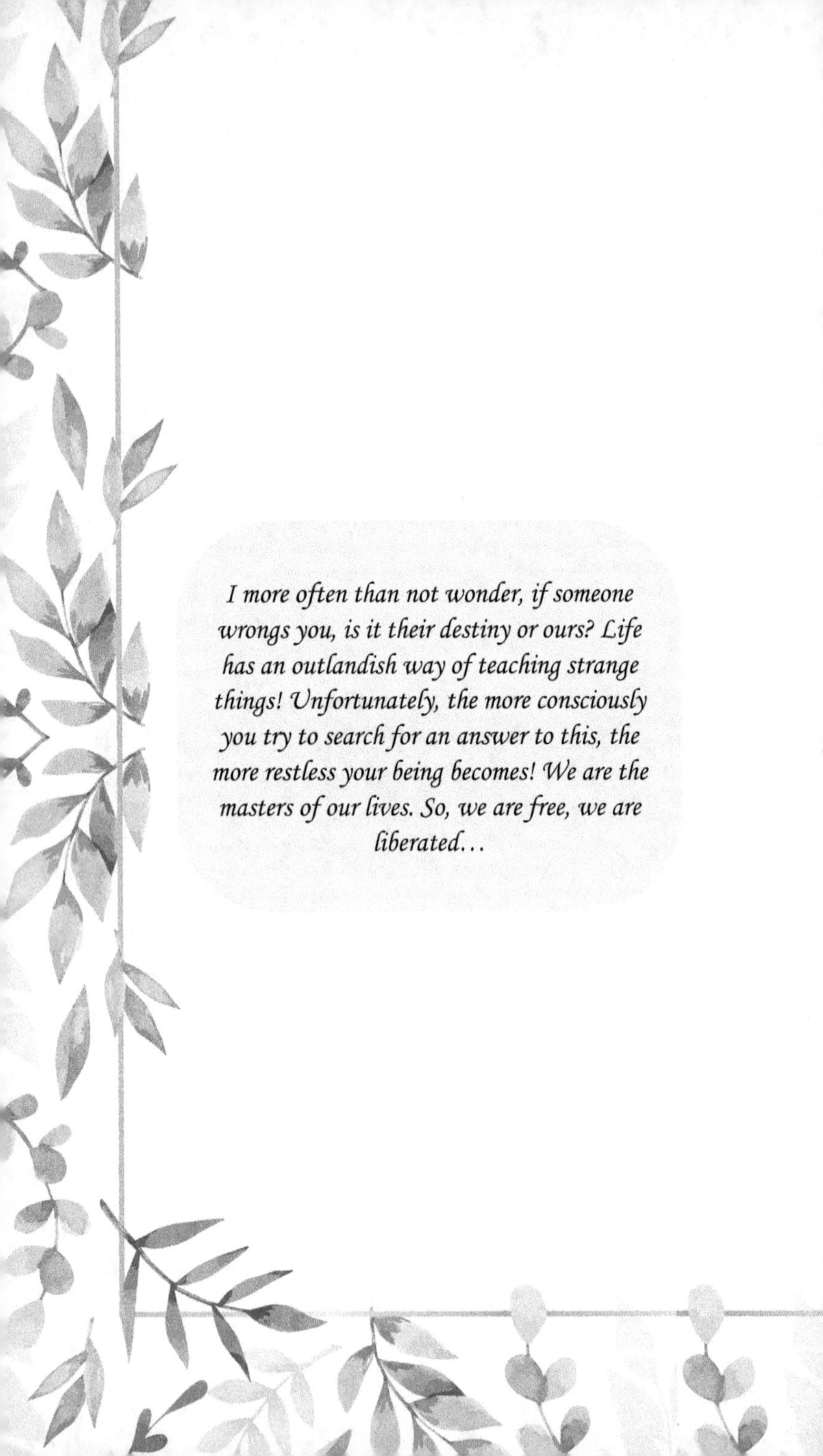

I more often than not wonder, if someone wrongs you, is it their destiny or ours? Life has an outlandish way of teaching strange things! Unfortunately, the more consciously you try to search for an answer to this, the more restless your being becomes! We are the masters of our lives. So, we are free, we are liberated…

Make each moment fortunate to spread your wings and let go of anything that weighs you down. Absorb yourself within the depths of your being and it unfurls how beautiful life – the gift from Him – is! Don't hold on to things that choke the celebration of this beautiful gift of life; for you are born to rejoice. Let go of anything and everything that's not part of YOU! Your life is your possession, then why let anyone decide its course. Don't blame anyone for any wrong they have done to you. For it was in that moment you realized how strong you are to let go and begin afresh. Thank them rather for lifting the veil of your strengths to you. Thank them for liberating you from the clutches of your transgressions, known or unknown. As long as your breaths are with your soul, you really have nothing, I repeat, nothing at all, to be wary of. Allow gratitude to unlock the fullness of life. Free yourself from the struggle to conquer the contour of your life and define your existence.

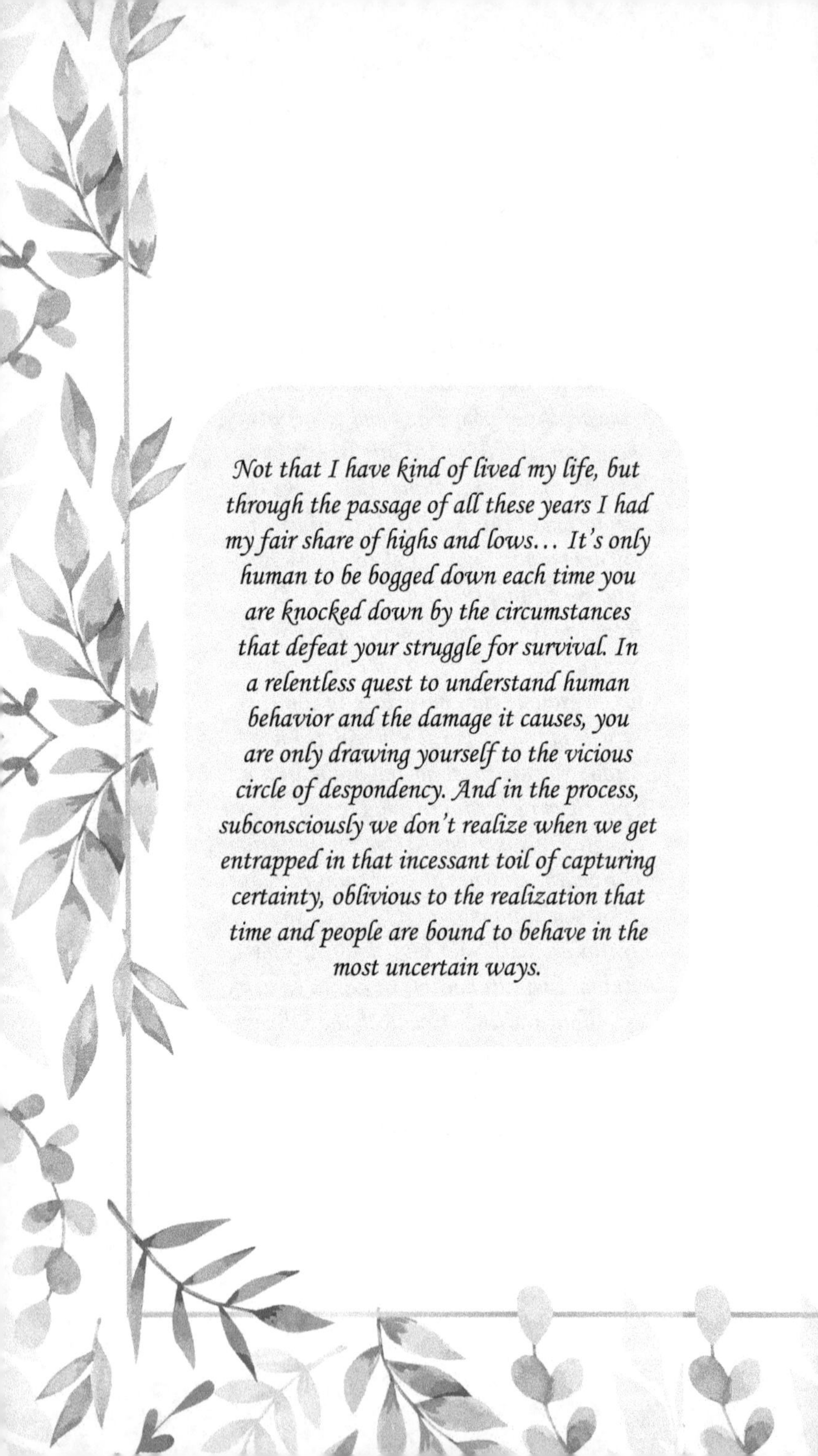

Not that I have kind of lived my life, but through the passage of all these years I had my fair share of highs and lows… It's only human to be bogged down each time you are knocked down by the circumstances that defeat your struggle for survival. In a relentless quest to understand human behavior and the damage it causes, you are only drawing yourself to the vicious circle of despondency. And in the process, subconsciously we don't realize when we get entrapped in that incessant toil of capturing certainty, oblivious to the realization that time and people are bound to behave in the most uncertain ways.

We have traveled lifetimes to be here… allow this to penetrate into our consciousness. Trust, the swallowing gloom is ephemeral, each time you rise like a phoenix, you only turn out to be stronger. Each time the adversities slow you down, create them as reminiscences that you will most cherish, for in adversities lie life's greatest opportunities. Take a deep breath and put an end to this avalanche of negativity. And it's only YOU who can do it. So, how about the thrill in exploring the unknown, the excitement, the sufferings, the tribulations and finally the quest and consequent emergence of a unique "You?" I have learned this the hard way, still synching though, that life like everything else is a zero-sum game, and the anguish and ordeal are a price we pay to meet the glories in the run-up to life.

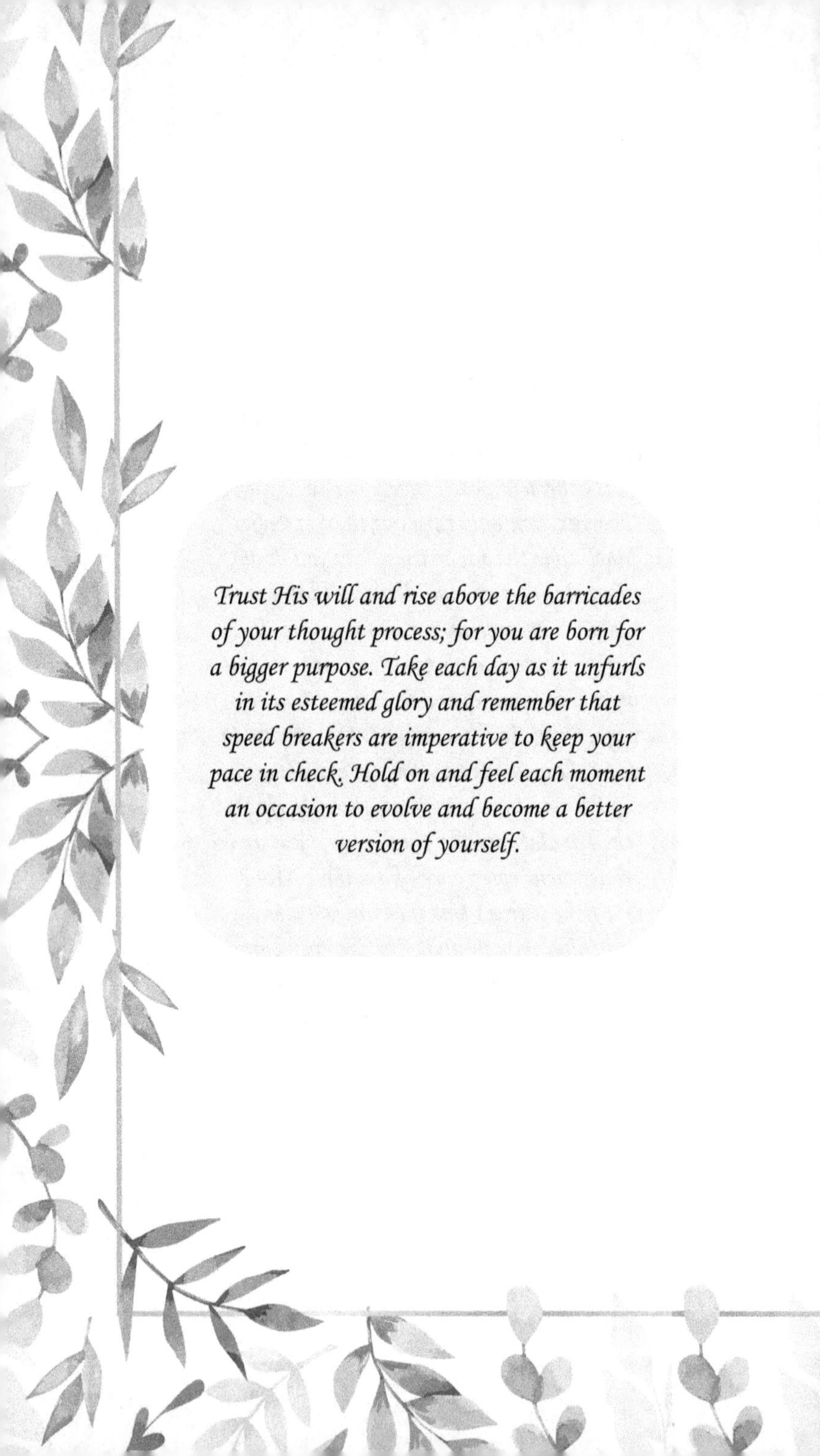

Trust His will and rise above the barricades of your thought process; for you are born for a bigger purpose. Take each day as it unfurls in its esteemed glory and remember that speed breakers are imperative to keep your pace in check. Hold on and feel each moment an occasion to evolve and become a better version of yourself.

The toughest battles are the ones which are against the closest ones.

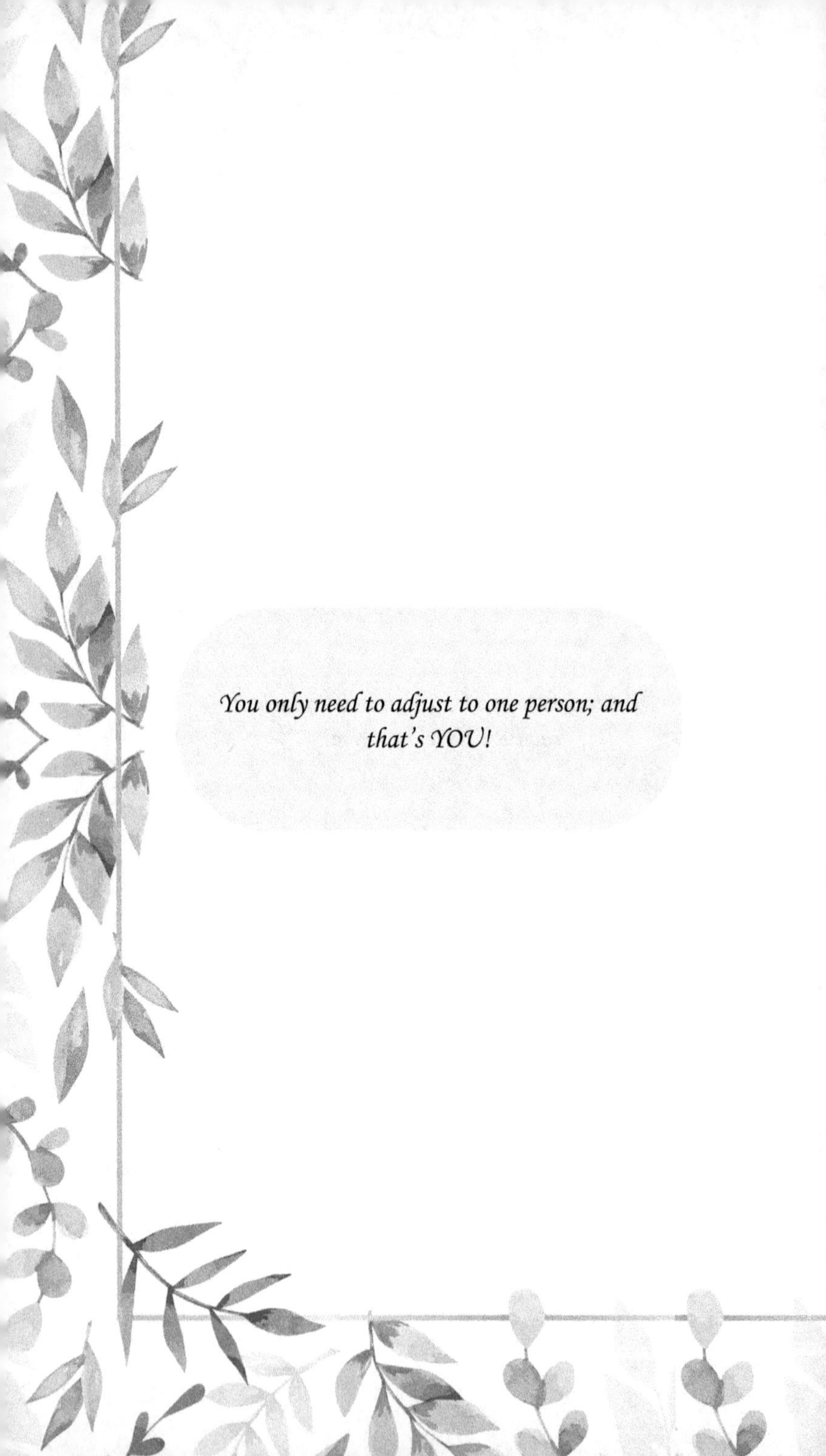

You only need to adjust to one person; and that's YOU!

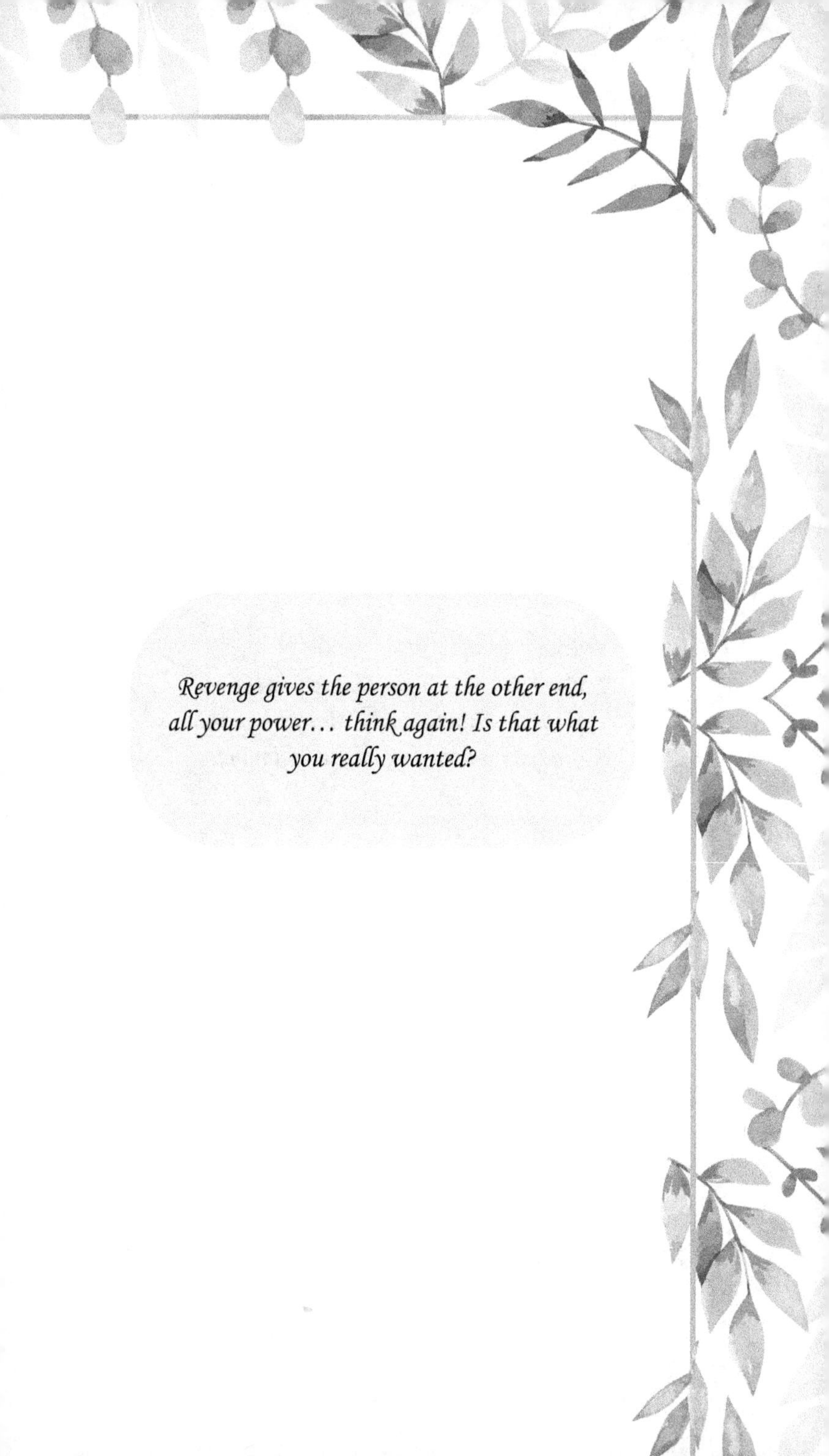

Revenge gives the person at the other end, all your power... think again! Is that what you really wanted?

Sometimes the night that marks the end of the day can be more beautiful than the day… a new day; a new beginning!

The ability to love sets a woman apart from a man.

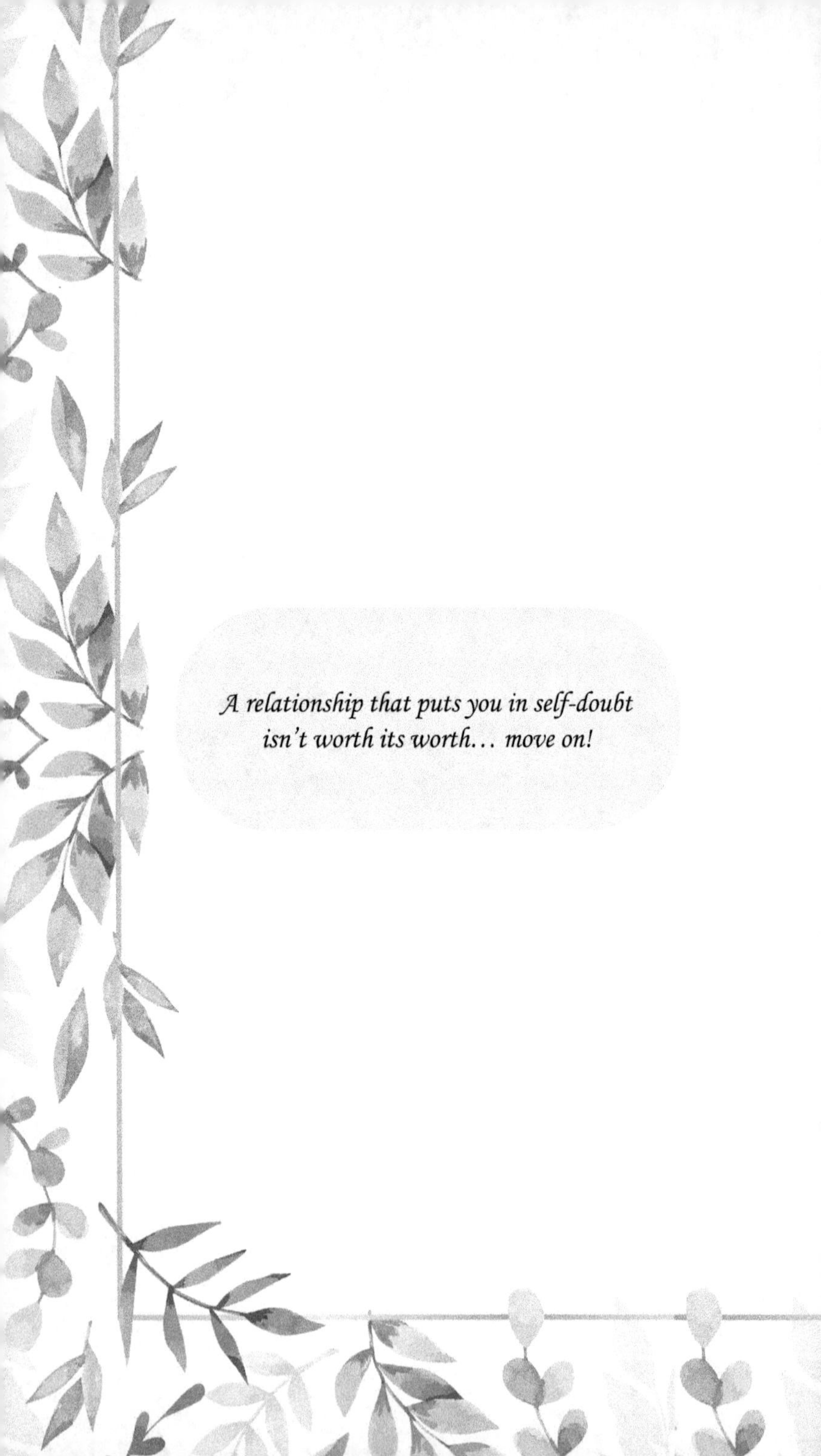

A relationship that puts you in self-doubt isn't worth its worth… move on!

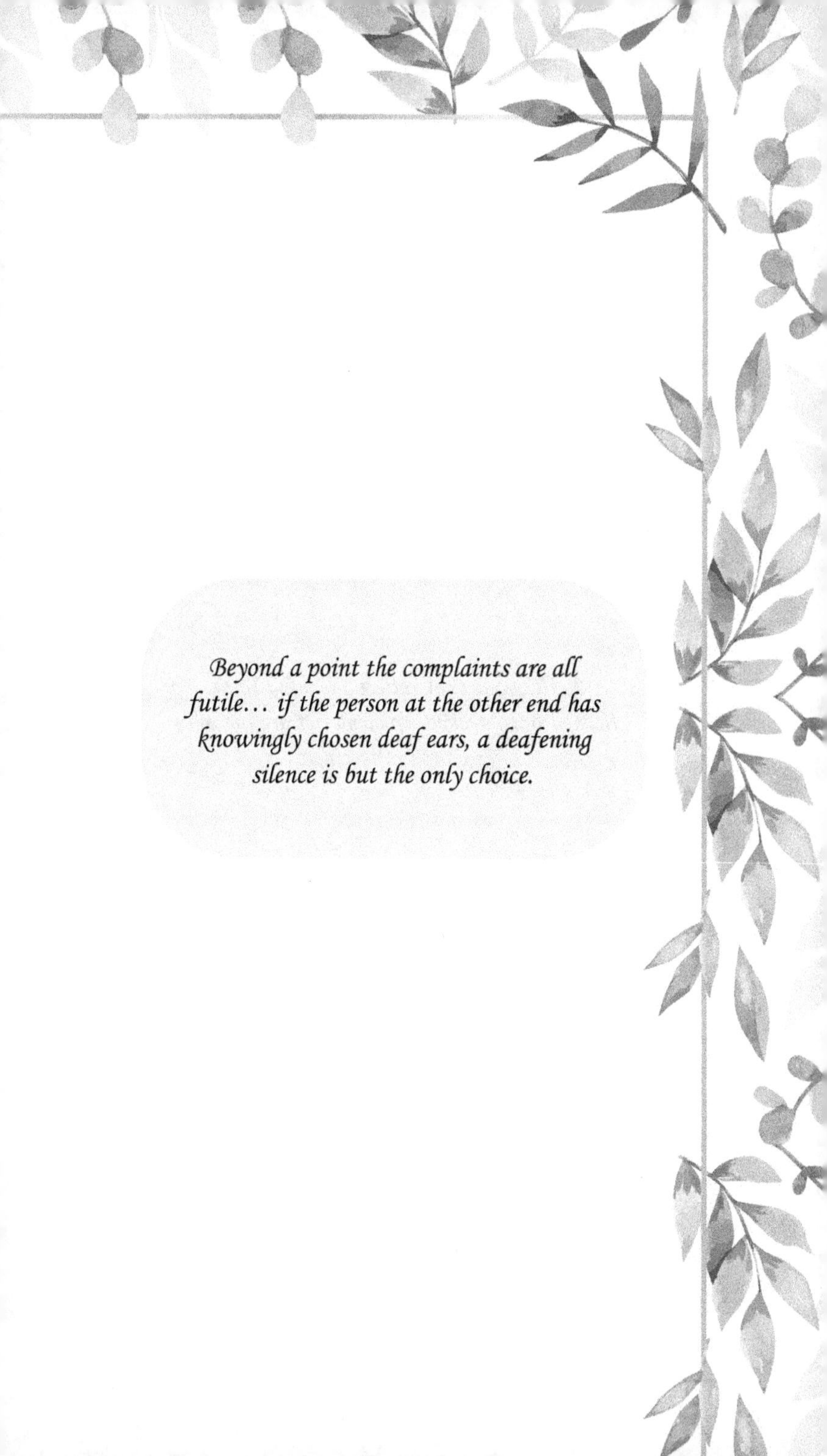

Beyond a point the complaints are all futile… if the person at the other end has knowingly chosen deaf ears, a deafening silence is but the only choice.

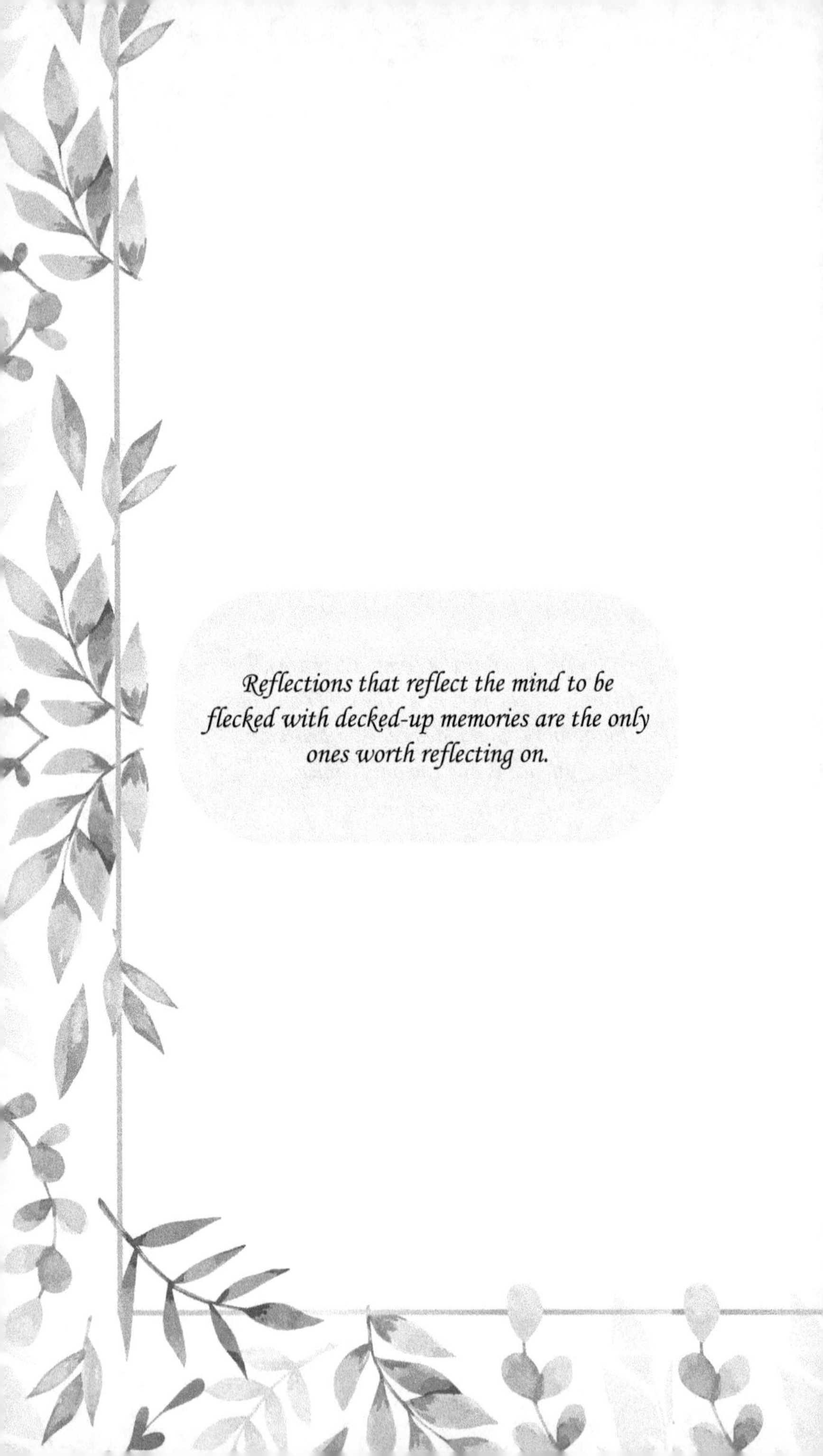

Reflections that reflect the mind to be flecked with decked-up memories are the only ones worth reflecting on.

On Soulmate…

The eyes that take you to you

The hands that hold you beyond you

The magic that sweeps you off the very you

The power that connects you to you

The felicity it induces in you

The elixir to love it brings in you

… that's the magic, the power to know you
more than you!

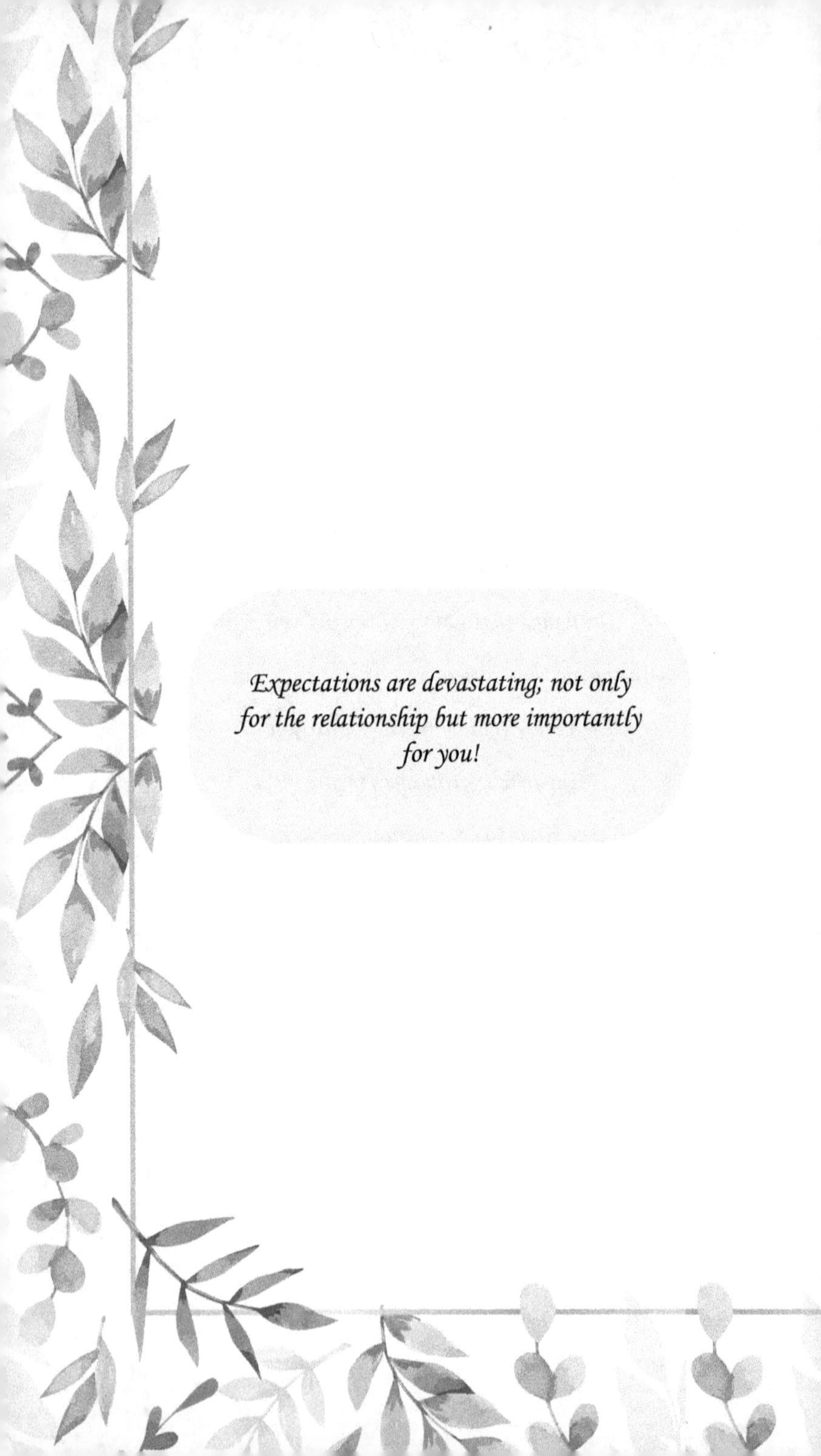

Expectations are devastating; not only for the relationship but more importantly for you!

Each day is a struggle, and struggle with no one else than those inner conflicts… deal with them one at a time; you aren't in any rat race.

It doesn't matter if you come out victorious or not… take it easy on yourself. The fact that you dealt with those suffices to determine you are a victorious warrior!

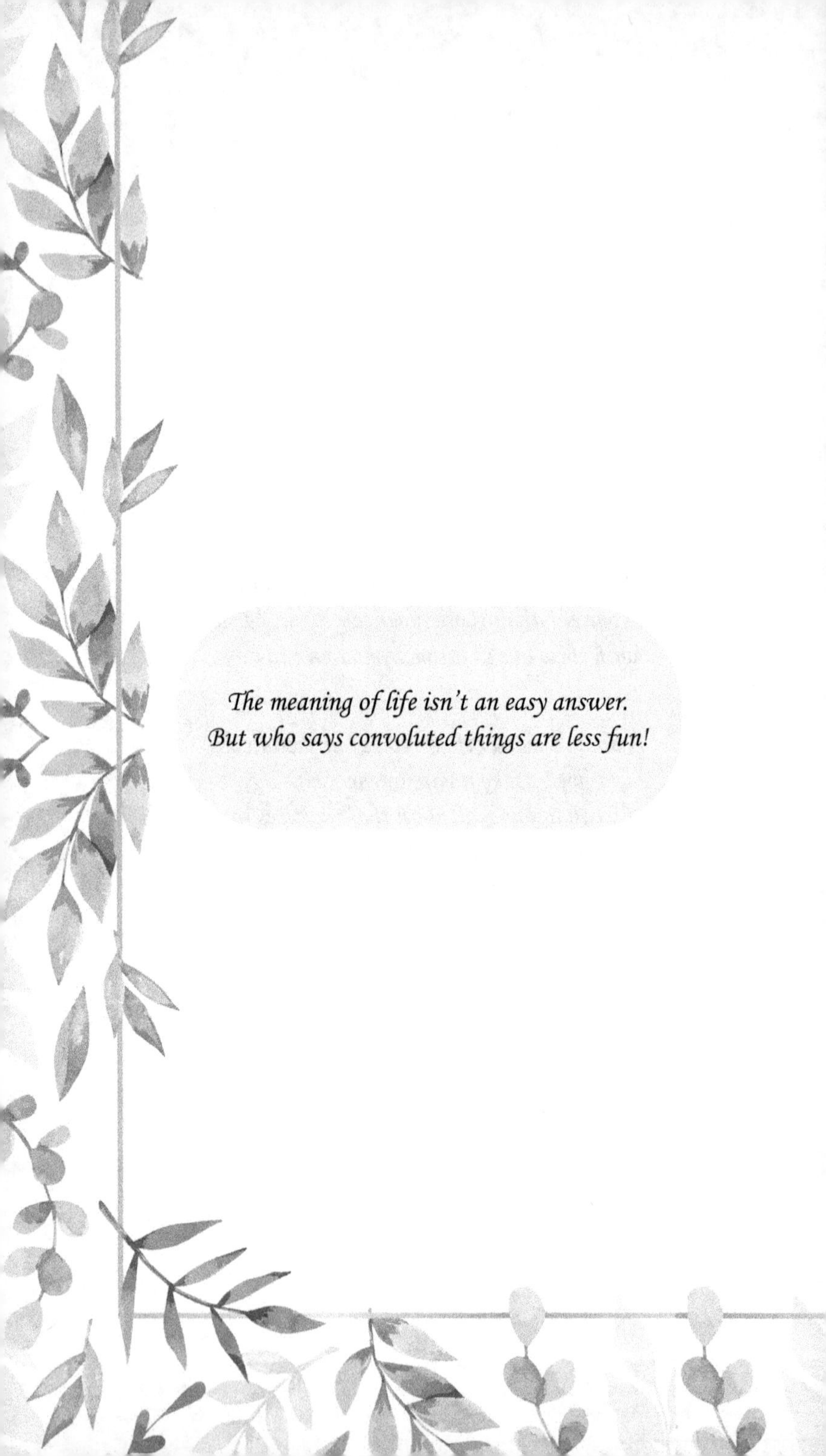

The meaning of life isn't an easy answer.
But who says convoluted things are less fun!

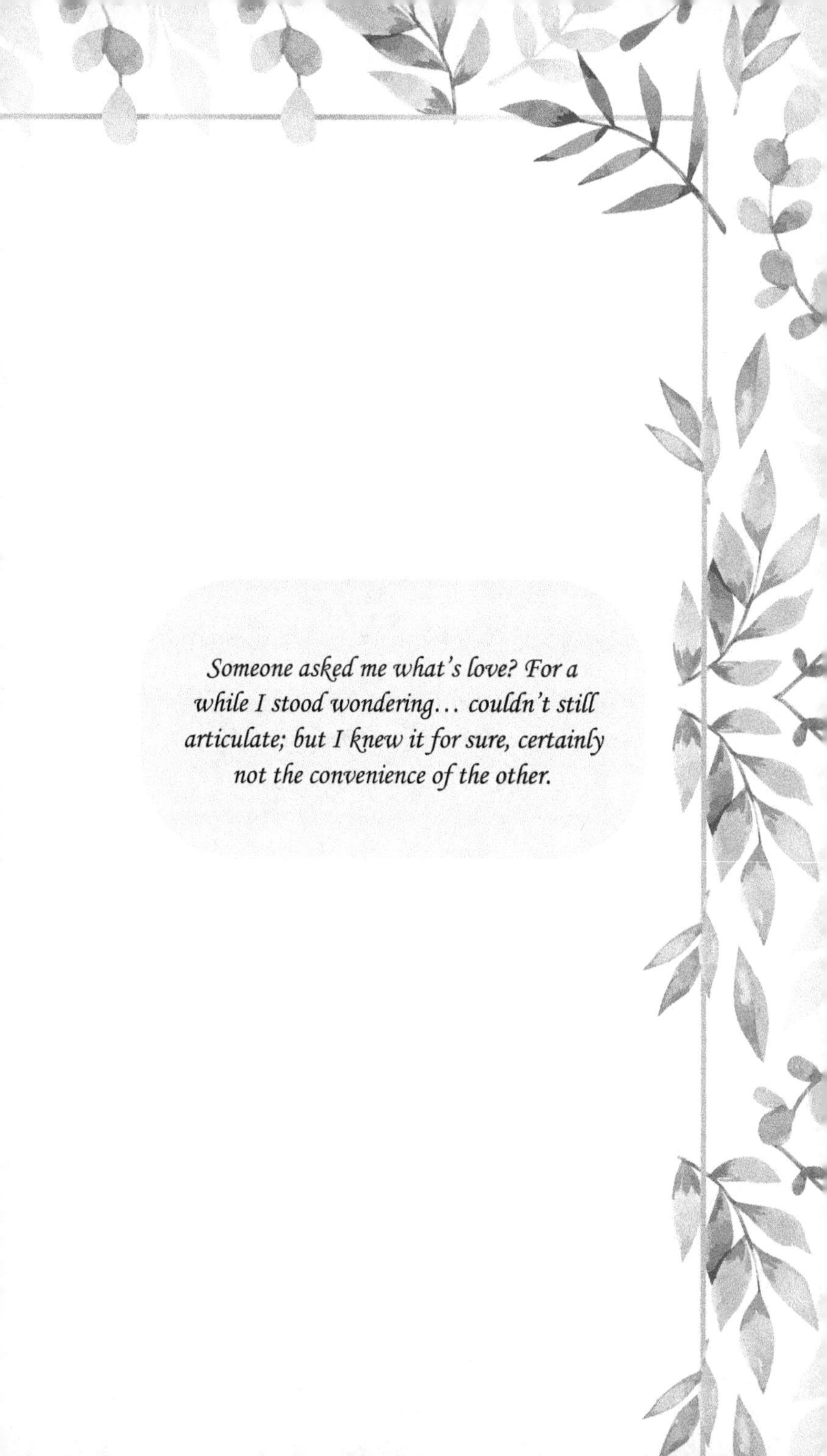

Someone asked me what's love? For a while I stood wondering… couldn't still articulate; but I knew it for sure, certainly not the convenience of the other.

Don't fear that fall; for it is not your call
Rise above that wall; and make it up for all

I like the dark skies better;
they take me deeper.

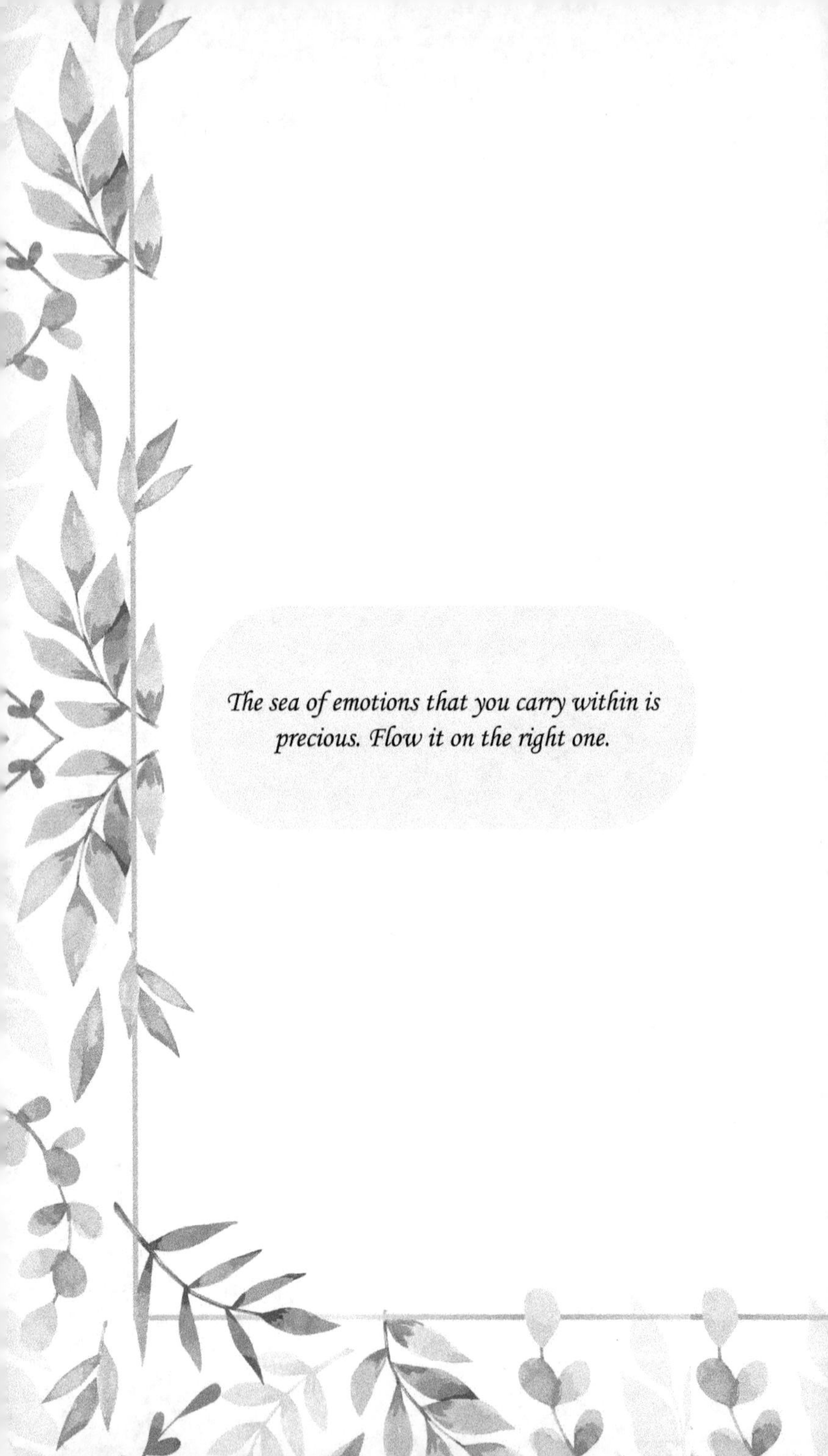

The sea of emotions that you carry within is precious. Flow it on the right one.

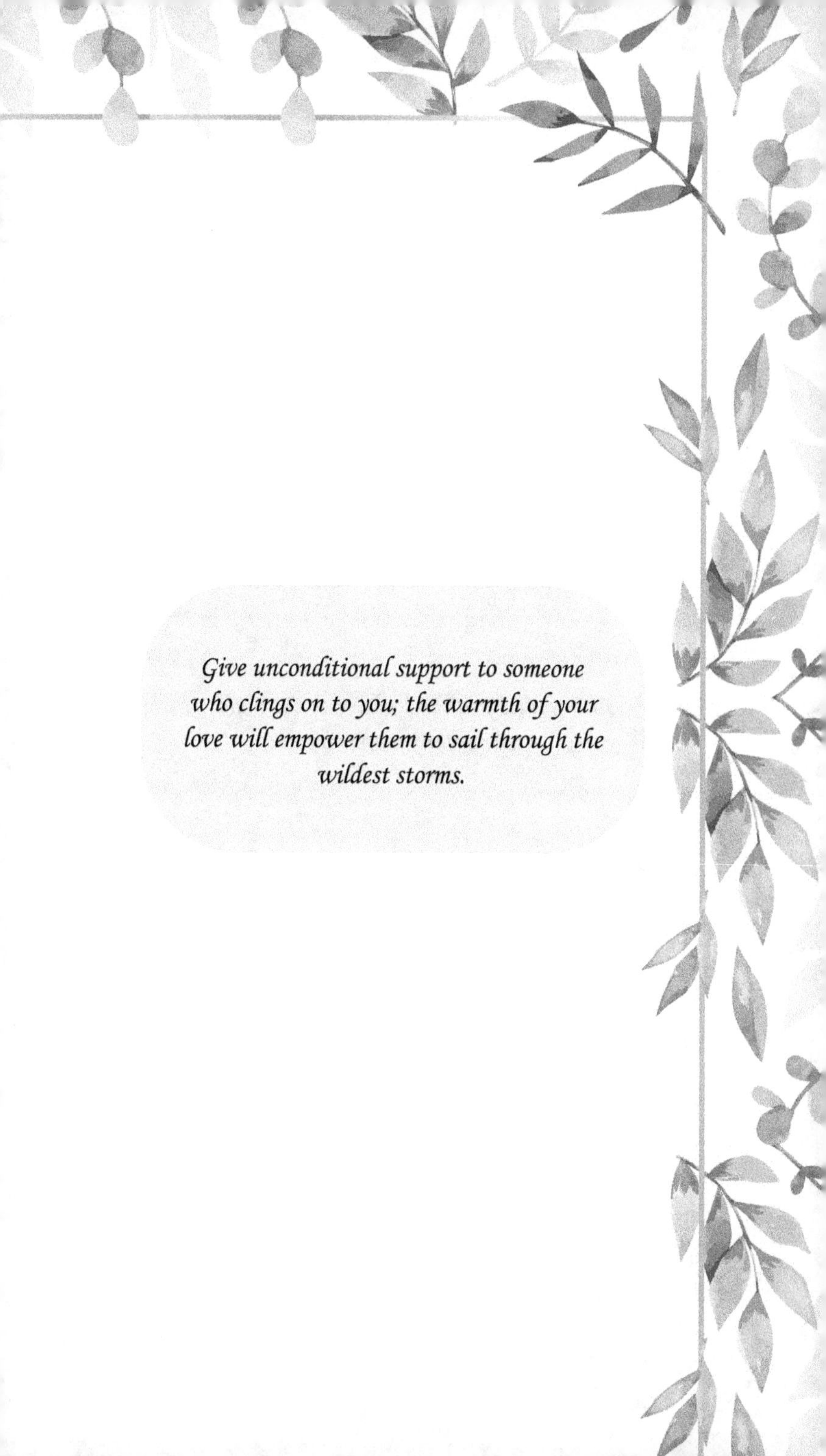

Give unconditional support to someone who clings on to you; the warmth of your love will empower them to sail through the wildest storms.

Lose yourself in the stillness of the night. It calms many storms inside.

When they mock you, don't be vengeful. Let it go… everyone writes their own karmas; you write yours well.

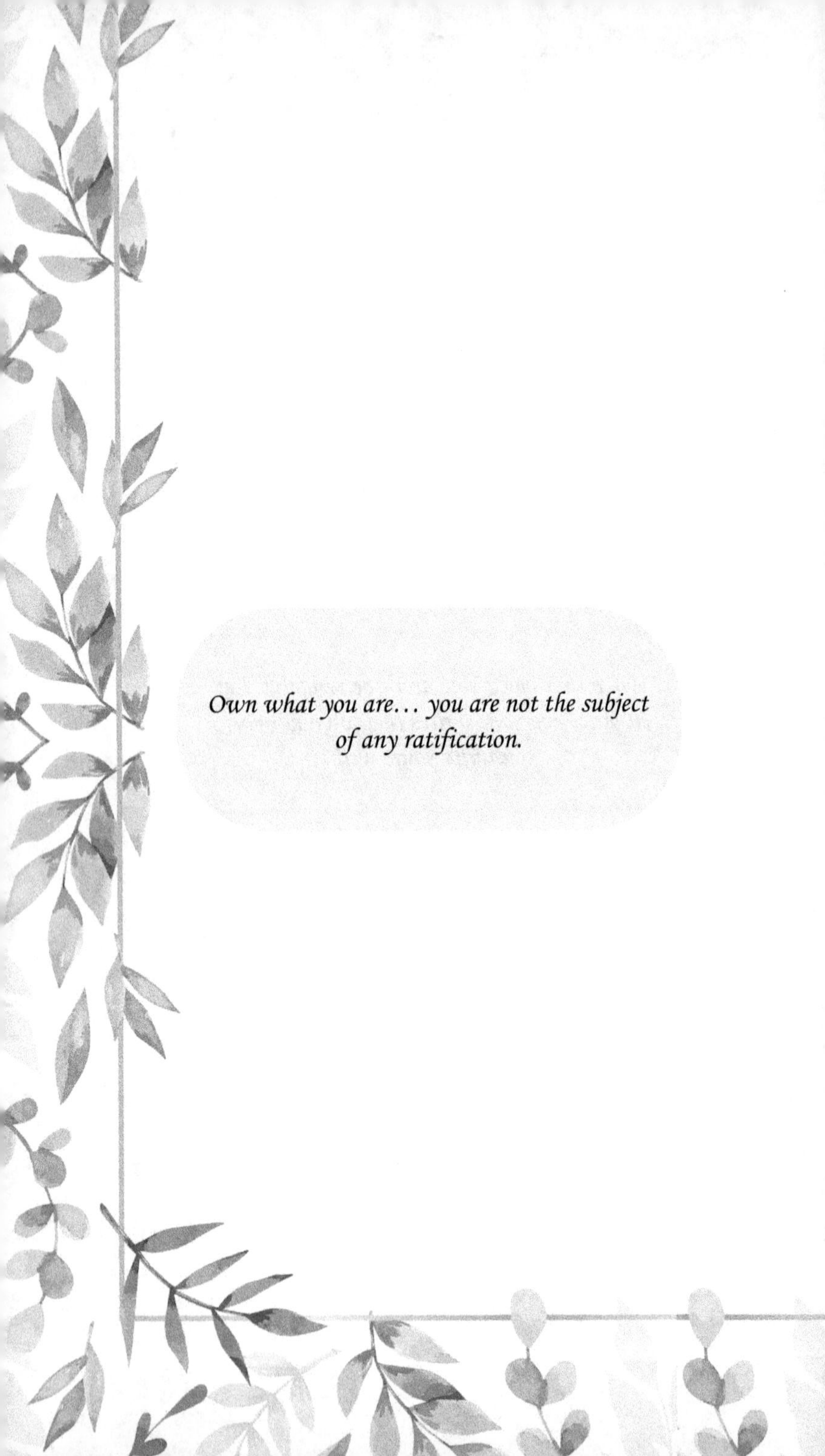

Own what you are… you are not the subject of any ratification.

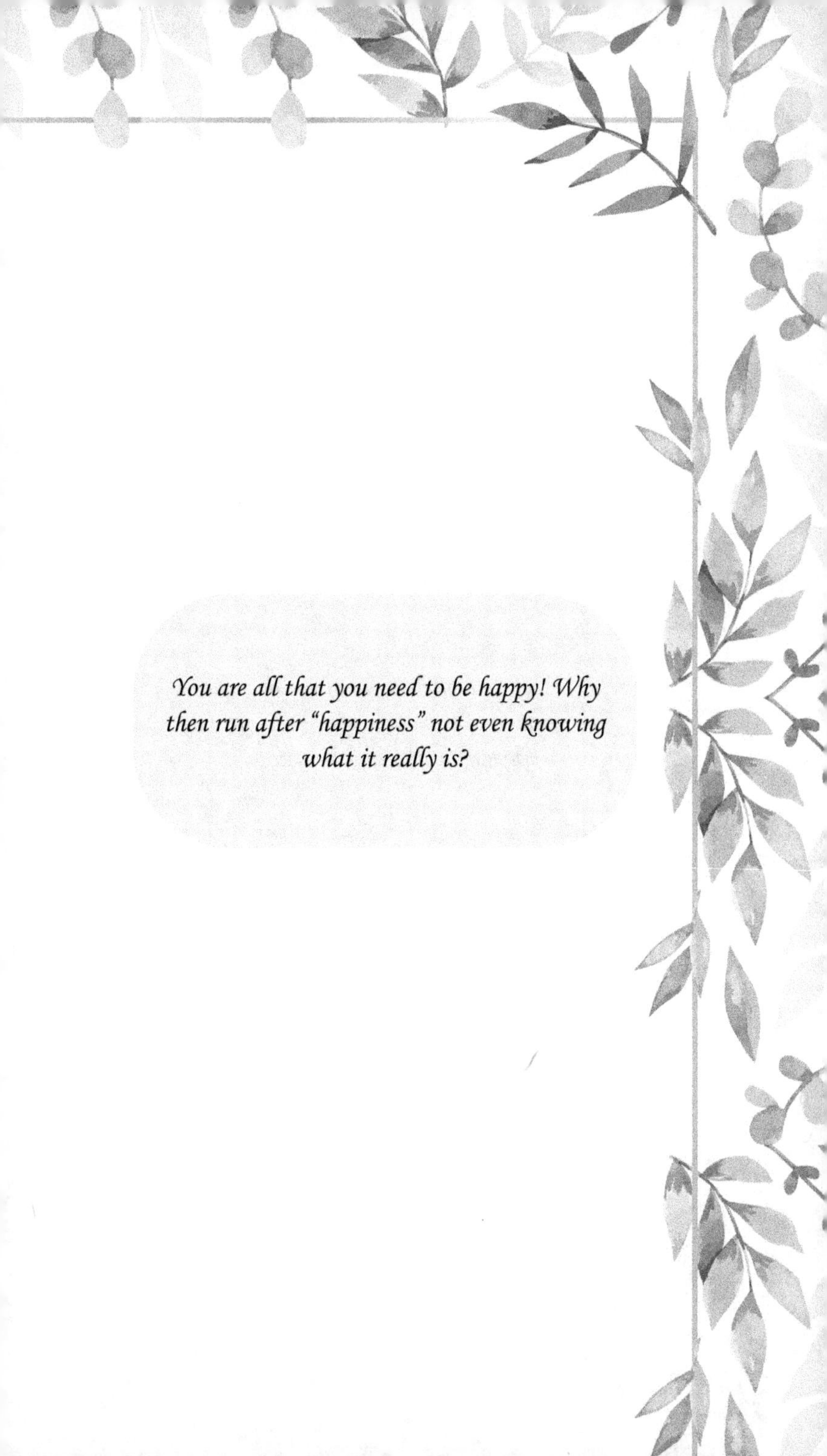

You are all that you need to be happy! Why then run after "happiness" not even knowing what it really is?

It's ok to look back, to grieve on some memories and rejoice on some. You are only human, let the emotions flow.

Stay away from those who bring out the worst in you!

The struggle to conquer a struggling mind is the toughest of all.

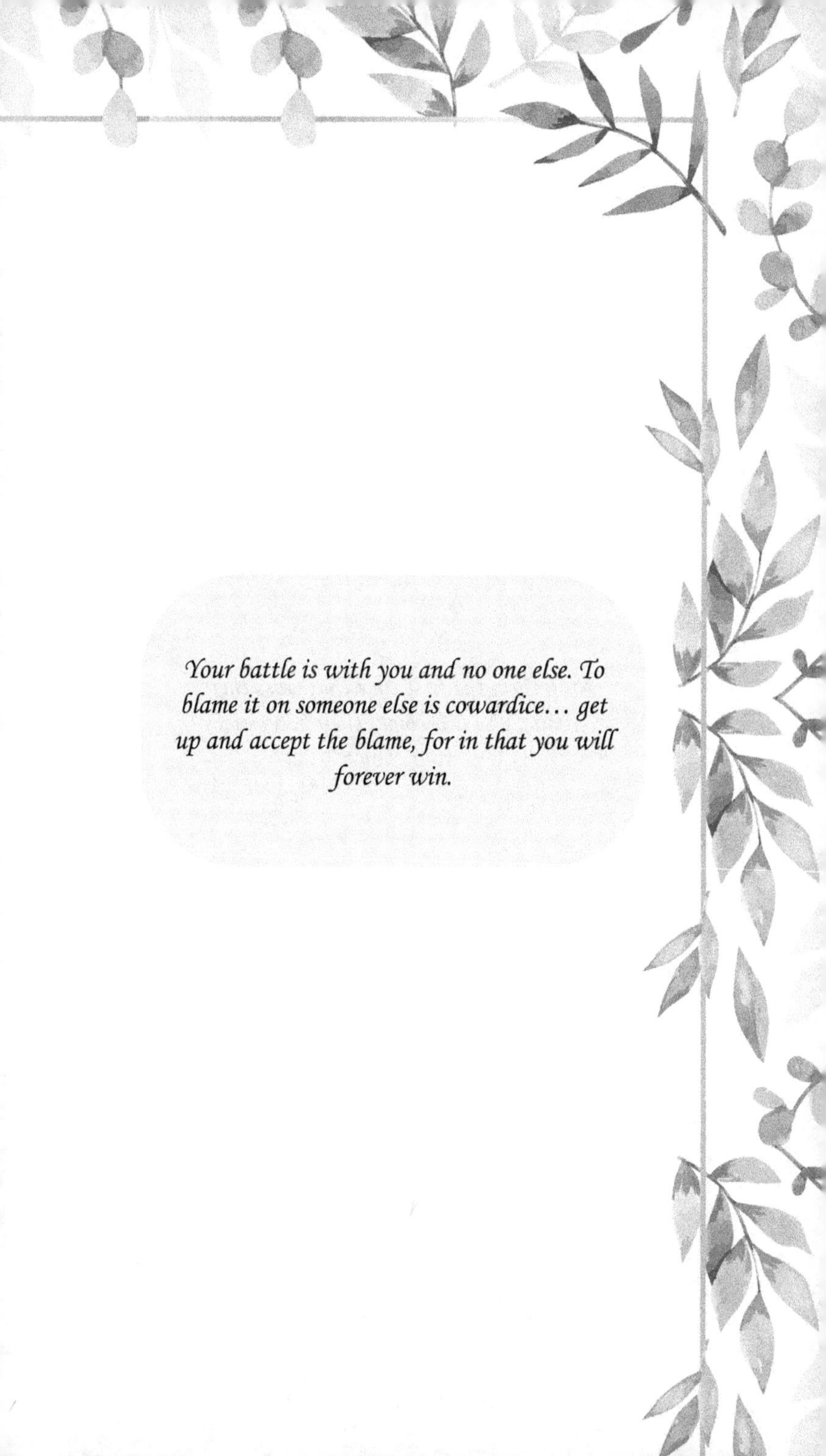

Your battle is with you and no one else. To blame it on someone else is cowardice… get up and accept the blame, for in that you will forever win.

Stop them the first time they cross their limits; else it becomes their habit and your choice.

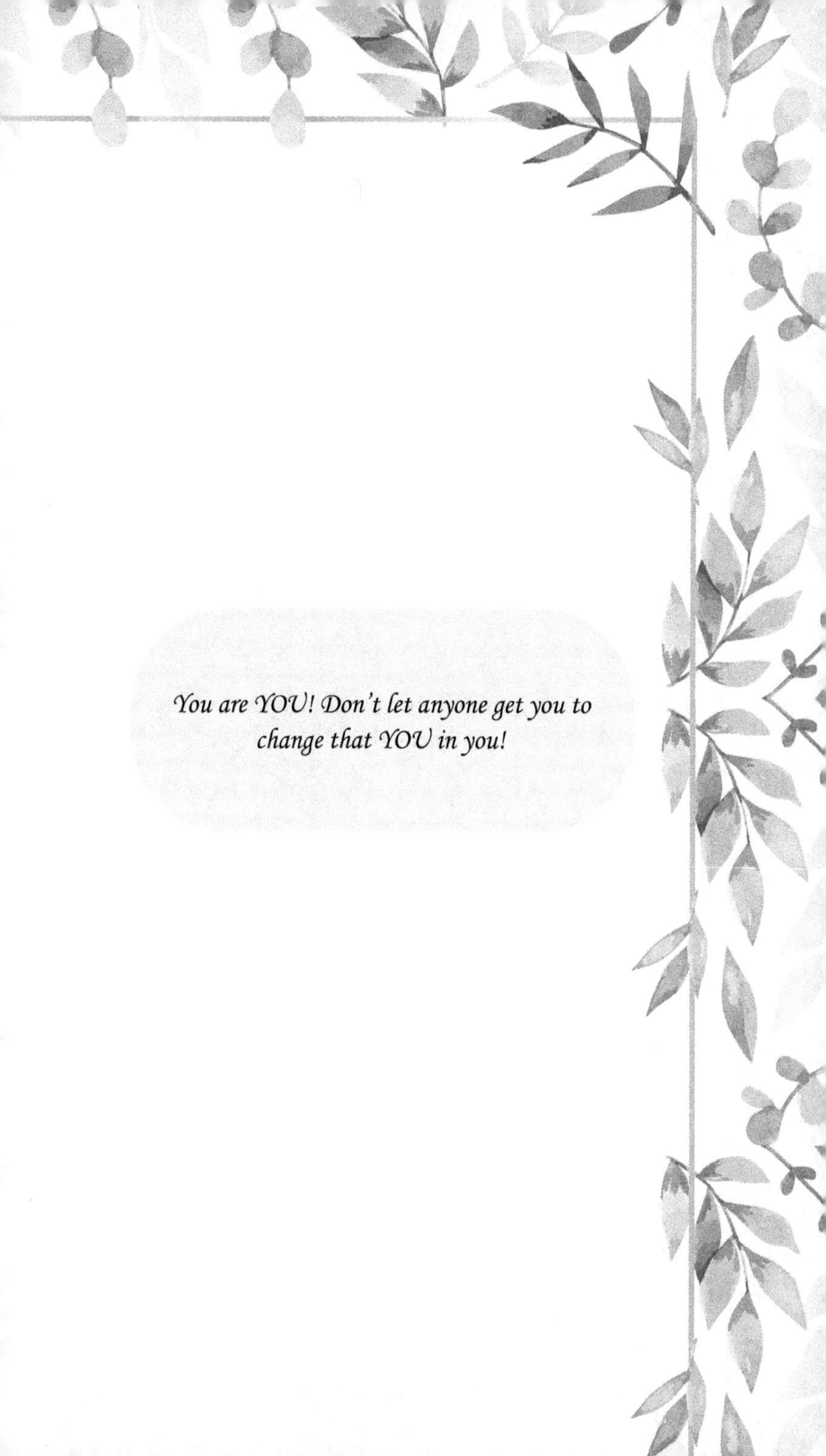

You are YOU! Don't let anyone get you to change that YOU in you!

Look me in the eye; I will take you to a new YOU!

Life!

Let go!

Live!

Let the child in you forever drive the adult in you.

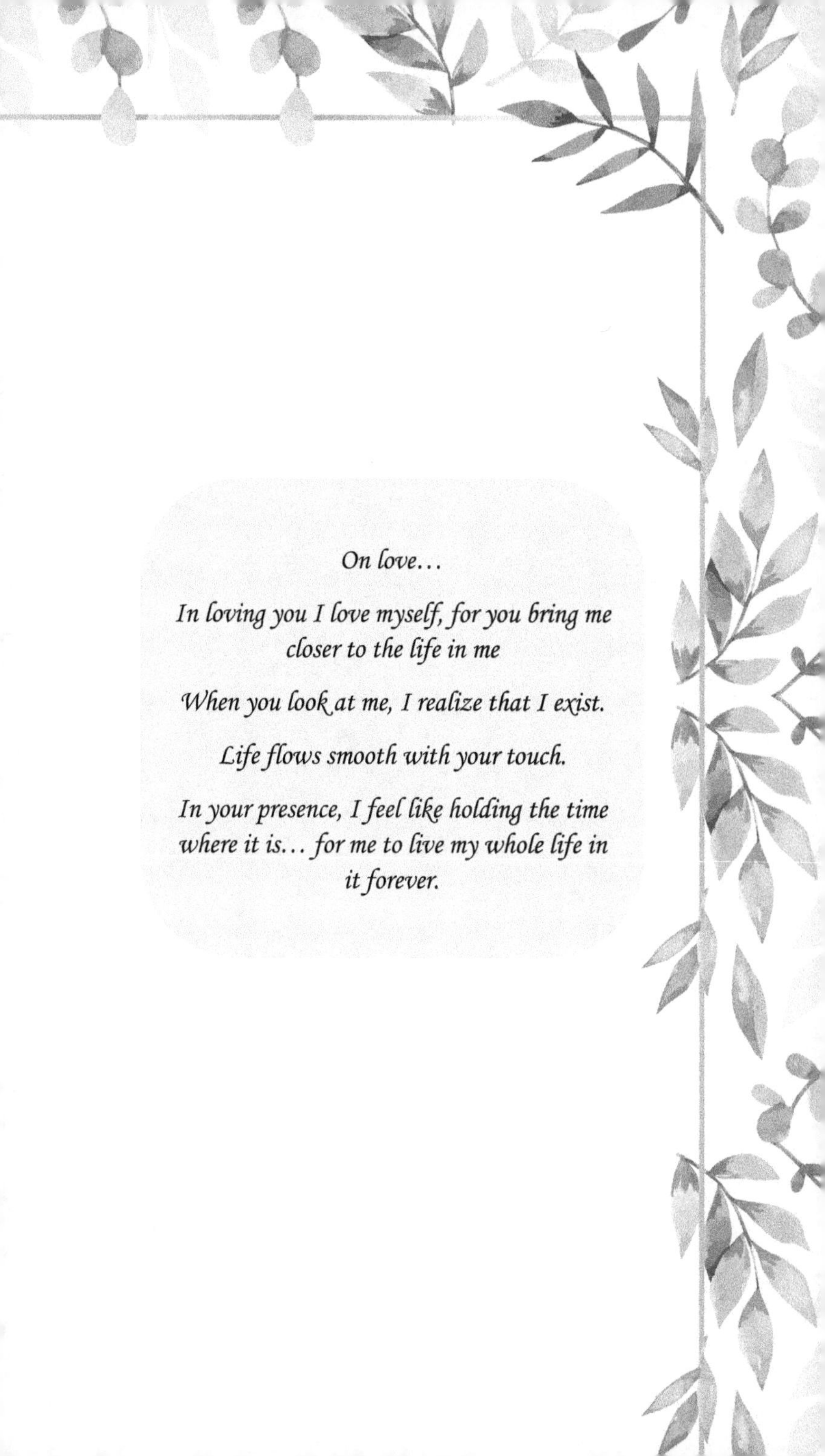

On love…

In loving you I love myself, for you bring me closer to the life in me

When you look at me, I realize that I exist.

Life flows smooth with your touch.

In your presence, I feel like holding the time where it is… for me to live my whole life in it forever.

Hope you rejoiced your journey as much as I did taking you through it!

Born and brought up in Delhi, Priyanka believes she is a quintessential contemporary Indian woman. She is a lawyer by profession, having a litigation background with several years of experience as a corporate lawyer. With a penchant for justice and equality, she completed her BA, LLB (Hons.), with 2nd rank from Amity Law School, Indraprastha University, and further did PG diploma courses in Corporate Law (1st rank) and Cyber Laws. She also holds a senior diploma in Hindustani classical music from the reputed Prayag Sangeet Samiti, Allahabad.

Apart from the years that she has spent as a corporate lawyer, she has also done photoshoots for Snapdeal and print-advertisement for a reputed jewelry brand. She has won the title of 'Mrs. Royal India Universe International 1st Princess 2018' in a beauty pageant for married women organized by Mrs. India Home Makers (MIHM) and has been crowned 'Mrs. Top Asia' at a global beauty pageant titled Woman of the Universe 2019. The pageant witnessed the participation of married women from across the globe and was held in October 2019 in the Dominican Republic. She has walked the ramp for many shows, the most prestigious one being the Lakmé Fashion Week in Mumbai in February 2020.

She has also been awarded 'Social Influencer and Corporate Lawyer' at the Women's Conclave and Award 2019, honoring the 51 most influential women, held in December 2019 in New Delhi.

Driven by her zeal for women's empowerment, she has been keenly involved in various activities, the most recent being the influencer, energy division for Womennovator, an initiative supported by the Ministry of Micro, Small and Medium Enterprises for providing a platform to women entrepreneurs.

Connect with Author:

Email: info@priyankadewan.co.in

Instagram: https://www.instagram.com/priyankadewan31

Facebook: https://www.facebook.com/priyanka.dewan.3591

Linkedin: https://www.linkedin.com/in/priyanka-dewan-6a065618a/

www.ingramcontent.com/pod-product-compliance
Lightning Source LLC
LaVergne TN
LVHW050545160826
845677LV00011B/2190

* 9 7 9 8 8 8 7 4 9 9 1 8 5 *